ARE YOU L

Your Worth

WITHDRAWN FROM STOCK

WITHDRAWN FROM STOCK

Over 100,000 copies of Tony Humphreys' books have already sold in the English language.

Books by Tony Humphreys

A Different Kind of Discipline
A Different Kind of Teacher
Examining Our Times
The Family: Love It and Leave It
Myself, My Partner
The Power of 'Negative' Thinking
Self-esteem: The Key to Your Child's Future
Work and Worth: Take Back Your Life

Audio-tapes and CDs by Tony Humphreys

Raising Your Child's Self-esteem
Self-esteem for Adults
Work and Self

WHOSE LIFE ARE YOU LIVING?
Realising Your Worth

Tony Humphreys

BA HDE, MA, PhD

Newleaf

Newleaf

an imprint of

Gill & Macmillan Ltd

Hume Avenue, Park West, Dublin 12

with associated companies throughout the world

www.gillmacmillan.ie

© Tony Humphreys 2003

0 7171 3662 0

Print origination by Type IT, Dublin

Printed by the Woodprintcraft Group Ltd, Dublin

This book is typeset in 11.5/15pt Rotis.

The paper used in this book comes from the wood pulp of managed forests. For every tree felled, at least one tree is planted, thereby renewing natural resources.

A CIP catalogue record for this book is available from the British Library.

5 4 3 2 1

CONTENTS

INTRODUCTION

You were not born bad, ugly, stupid, slow, average, superior, inferior, depressed, anxious, useless, obsessive-compulsive, delusional, paranoid, aggressive, violent, passive, shy, timid, fearful, emotionless. Nevertheless, these are just some of the labels with which adults describe themselves or are described by others. Furthermore, apart from congenital physical conditions, the majority of us were not born sick; nonetheless, the rate of illness among adults is considerable.

Freedom to live one's own life is a universal aspiration. The aspiration begs the question: What is it that is stopping you from being authentic? You may answer: 'My parents or my boss or the church or my wife or my husband or society or my children.' However, as an adult what mostly blocks you from being real is yourself.

 No matter where you are, what you are feeling, how you are behaving, whether you are rich or poor, educated or poorly educated, employed or unemployed, married or single, atheist or theist, well or sick, young or old, living or dying, you have a self that is sacred, unique and ingenious. Sadly, a long, long time ago you began to hide away many or all aspects of your real self behind a screen, a façade of thoughts, feelings, words and actions. Depending on the level and intensity of the threats to your expression of your unique self, you may have lost either partial or total touch with your real self. However, there is a part of you that not only knows everything that has happened to you, but remains in touch with your sacred presence – this is your unconscious mind.

From your earliest days you actively found means to hide your real self from family, social, religious, political and educational forces that pressurised you to conform to their ways. These pressures accelerated as you got older. Whether young or old, demands that get you to suppress or repress your own spontaneity and wisdom lead to a crust being formed around your core self. You knew as a child and know now as an adult the dangers of living your own life. Examples of past and present pressures are:

- 'Do as I say.'
- 'Stay away from there.'
- 'Don't touch things.'
- 'Sit still.'
- 'Don't think like that.'
- 'Stand up for yourself.'
- 'For God's sake hurry up.'
- 'Speak slowly.'
- 'Shape up.'
- 'Don't be stupid.'
- 'Don't let us down.'
- 'Stop making a fool of yourself.'
- 'You mustn't feel like that.'

When shaken, hurt or abandoned, in order to survive you fashioned a false persona, a shadow self that would satisfy the expectations of others, particularly the significant people in your life. For the sake of conformity you hid away some or all aspects of your real self. In the place of your unique self — naturally intuitive, harmonious, different, dynamic and highly intelligent — a foreign self has been substituted. You do not rest easily with this false persona; in your innermost place you want to express your own true self. You may say, 'Conformity is reality; that is how things are and there is nothing anybody can do about it.' But I believe that the very resources you employed to hide away your true self can be employed equally to bring forward the light of your real self. Even though it is neither an easy nor a short journey, it is exciting and the prize is possession and expression of your sacred self no matter where you are, whom you are with or what you are doing. You will see things in yourself that up to now you dared not allow even yourself to touch into.

Contemporary society worships at the altar of success, and 'having' has become the sinister enemy of 'being'. Our lives are pressurised and stressful because we have lost conscious sight of our true nature. Each day becomes a deeper hiding of our real selves. We depend on our parents, spouses, friends, lovers, children, employers to make us feel good, and when they fail us, we turn to medical, psychiatric, psychological and other helping practitioners. We entrust ourselves to others and are prepared to burden others with our lives, to the detriment of their well-being. Furthermore, when we give over responsibility to social systems, these organisations very often collude with our helplessness by primarily reassuring us and thereby repressing us.

Ask yourself the question: Whose life are you living? Are you living the life of your parents, your spouse, your employer, your lover, your children, your church? By giving up your freedom, you no longer belong to yourself. You belong to the powers and people who have lessened and demeaned your presence.

You need to belong to yourself. As you learn to deepen your contact with your unique self, you will discard the façades, the pseudo-images, the masks, the disguises and postures that have served to protect you but also prevented expression of your authenticity. Illnesses — for example, infections, colds, flu, stomach and bowel problems, tension and

migraine headaches, back pain, high or low blood pressure —
that were needed to reduce emotional and social threats will
either be eliminated or reduced. You will discover your
individuality, dynamism and vast capability to live your life
from the inside out.

No matter what age you are, you can bring the light of your
real self forward and emerge from the darkness that has
hidden you.

PART ONE
SELF BEFORE THE ECLIPSE

CHAPTER ONE
YOUR REAL SELF

IN THE BEGINNING WAS THE LIGHT

At a graduation ceremony for counsellors, some of the relatives of the graduates had brought babies in arms. While awaiting my turn to speak, I observed the audience of adults, children and infants. Everyone except the infants sat quietly, obediently listening to the speakers. Whilst not unduly intrusive, the babies 'aahed' and 'oohed', looked around them and gleefully responded to attention from their minders. Their curiosity and excitement was a thrill to watch. When it came to my turn to speak, I remarked, 'how wonderful it is to have some free and confident voices in the hall, and I am not talking about the adults.' I also expressed the wish that these babies would not lose their spontaneity, because my work in clinical psychology often involves helping adults, adolescents and children to rediscover their own voice.

Except for those babies who experience physical or emotional threats in the womb, infants are an amazing source of light in the often dark world of the people they encounter and the cultures they inhabit. Watch them — they are unique, spontaneous, naturally curious, adventurous, able to give and receive love, sure, poised, confident and remarkably good at making their needs known. They love life, are harmonious, vociferous, gentle, sensitive, expressive and separate. They are uninhibited; they enjoy their bodies and do not allow failure to block their progress, nor are they seduced by success. On the contrary, they trip, they fall, they

1

fail to execute an action, they succeed, but they keep moving on to the next challenge. Progress is what drives them forward. Infants also enjoy time on their own and are masters at amusing themselves. What a contrast this picture of infants is to that of adults and older children, whose typical profile includes being inhibited, fear of failure, dependence on success, guardedness, difficulty in either giving or receiving love, worry about the approval of others, low risk-taking, lack of confidence, shyness, timidity, fear, aggression, insecurity and possessiveness. What happened to our light and how to become re-enlightened are the themes of this book.

The presence of each infant is unique, sacred and unrepeatable and takes expression in multiple ways — physical, emotional, intellectual, behavioural, social, sexual, creative and spiritual.

PHYSICAL EXPRESSION OF PRESENCE

Every infant has a unique physical presence and is different in size, shape, colour, skin texture, movement, bodily expression and physical intelligence — the infant's body knows when hunger and thirst are there and not there, and the foods that best suit physical development. The infant's body will rest and sleep when necessary and be active when energised.

No matter what movement, facial expression, body posture or illness symptom the infant shows, it is important that parents and others see that these physical manifestations are always right. The baby may be communicating hunger, thirst, physical discomfort, need for attention, depression, need for stimulation, fear of abandonment, anxiety, excitement, sickness. Furthermore, physical explorations of their own bodies and those of parents, as well as of their physical environment, are all intelligent attempts by infants to know the physical worlds they encounter.

EMOTIONAL EXPRESSION OF PRESENCE

When it comes to emotional expression and receptivity, babies have been seriously maligned. For too long, infants have been seen as egocentrics who believe the world revolves around them. My own observations and the reports of parents, particularly mothers, suggest the opposite. Not only are babies good at receiving love, they are equally involved in giving love. I believe that when babies reach up to adults, they do so to be loved and to give love. Love is a two-sided coin, and all human beings have an innate drive to love and be loved.

In the same way that the infant's body is always right, so too are the infant's feelings. Feelings are generally regarded by most psychologists as the most accurate barometer of what is happening to a person at any one moment in time. Whilst I agree with this belief, I also contend that every bodily movement, thought, action, dream, sound or creation is an equally powerful and accurate expression of a person's present state of well-being.

Babies can demonstrate a range of feelings that reflect the presence of inner security: contentment, affection, peaceful-ness, excitement, joy, wonder, humour. When insecure, as a result of hunger, thirst, pain or threat, they manifest feelings such as fear, alarm, frustration, anger, rage, grief, sadness, depression, apathy. It is vital that these wonderful emergency feelings of infants are responded to immediately so that the dark clouds of unmet needs do not gather. I call these feelings 'emergency feelings', as they are an attempt to alert the self and others to the presence of some threat, real or perceived, and they need caring and effective responses.

Not only are infants marvellous at emotional expression, they are equally impressive when it comes to emotional receptivity. Babies are wonderfully receptive to affection, warmth and fun, and will very quickly pick up tension, crossness, anger, uncertainty, nervousness, frustration or depression in the adults who take care of them. Whilst the presence or expression of emergency feelings in adults puts babies' security under threat, compared to adults they are unconditionally loving, understanding and quick to show love when their distressed carers are ready to receive it. No enduring sulk or withdrawal or aggression results; a willingness to return to a state of equilibrium is always present.

INTELLECTUAL EXPRESSION OF PRESENCE

The intellectual expression of infants has been gravely underestimated, mainly because of our society's confusion of intelligence with knowledge. One of the first challenges that infants face is learning the foreign verbal and non-verbal language of their carers. They do this in an amazingly short time and without any formal education. Moreover, during that learning process they have their own physical language, which they employ ingeniously to communicate their needs. They also learn to read the body language of adults. In contrast to adults, infants are highly developed in reading non-verbal communication.

Of course, it takes babies time to build up knowledge of the physical, familial, social, educational, religious, political, sexual, emotional and creative worlds they have been born into, but they possess an incredible capacity to make sense and order out of these complex worlds. They also have a natural curiosity and an eagerness to learn. It is in these early years that human beings learn more about the world than at any subsequent time.

BEHAVIOURAL EXPRESSION OF PRESENCE

Behavioural expression is the baby's attempts to learn the skills required to survive and progress in the social systems they inhabit. Their behavioural repertoire will always reflect the culture and sub-cultures of which they are members. For example, babies born to traditional Javanese families rarely, if ever, cry; they do not need to as their carers detect their needs at a much earlier stage of expression. In Java, infants are physically carried for the first twelve months of their life and the language of tension in their bodies, or restlessness or coldness or rushes of heat, is picked up in the physical closeness with their carers. Western babies have to resort to the more urgent voice of crying to get their needs seen and met.

What is astounding is how speedily infants adapt behaviourally to the settings in which they live. They also learn to read the faces and eyes, bodily movements, tone of voice and body posture of adults, and they choose protective actions to reduce any threat that is present.

As with feelings, every behaviour a child exhibits always makes sense. No action on the part of a child is stupid, negative, nonsensical or insane. But many adults are not in a position to appreciate the wisdom of infants, and for their own protective reasons they choose to react harshly to certain behavioural expressions of their offspring. Key opportunities to deepen the security of children are missed when parents have lost the realisation that all human behaviour makes sense.

Much has been made of children's capacity to imitate adults, but what is often not seen is that such responses are creative attempts to get to know and adapt to their outer worlds. Not to adapt would mean appearing alien, and babies are not fools when it comes to knowing what the consequences of this could mean. A clear distinction needs to be made between intuition and learning. Intuition is an innate knowing that puts infants on the alert when any threat to their well-being is present. Learning arises in response to the intuitive knowing of what range of behaviours would serve infants best in their home and other environments. Infants are well ahead of adults in acting out from an intuitive place.

Infants and young children also put adults to shame when it comes to honesty, spontaneity and openness. One four-year-old's mother continually complained that she never had any free time. She was astounded when her little daughter said with some exasperation: 'Mum, I think you're going to be dead before you find free time.' How accurate was the child's observation. Another story involves a single woman in her mid-thirties who was attending a family function, which also included her young niece. This woman's brothers and sisters, all married with children, were being photographed in their separate family groups, but no suggestion of photographing the unmarried sister was made. Much to the woman's embarrassment, her little niece very assertively insisted that her aunt be photographed on her own. What a pity it took the child to make the adults aware of the importance of affirming each person's particular state of living.

Adults often do not see that each child in a family will find a unique way to behaviourally express self. Apparently, when I was a baby, my twin brother would continue to suck his empty bottle, whereas as soon as mine was empty I would pitch it out of the cot. As we grew older the behavioural differences became more marked. He became an expert at extroversion, humour, creating friendships, charm and roguery, whereas I became more academic, homebound, caring of others, introverted, shy and honest.

SOCIAL EXPRESSION OF PRESENCE

Have you ever noticed that in a group of people which includes a baby, the person whose social presence stands out and attracts most attention is often that of the baby? This phenomenon is not due to the obligatory noises adults make around the newcomer. No, there is an ancient recognition present, a suppressed or repressed memory of adults' own infant experience of freedom to express fully one's presence. There is the added factor that a baby's aura radiates a healthy and non-threatening invitation to make contact. The social presence of the infant is unique, special, unrepeatable, individual, beautiful, self-contained and wonderfully expressive of and receptive to unconditional attention. Invariably each baby finds their own way to make their presence felt – the smile, the eye contact, the peaceful countenance, clapping, pulling, rocking, sighs, 'cute' mannerisms, attraction to colours, shiny objects – no end of ways.

The light of infants' social presence is maintained when others around them worship their unique presence and do not compare them with others, but rather celebrate their difference.

SEXUAL EXPRESSION OF PRESENCE

In contrast to many older children, adolescents and adults, toddlers demonstrate great comfort and ease with their bodies and are not shy in exploring and experiencing pleasure from their erogenous zones.

Their sexual expression is natural and is not split off from the other aspects of their being, as it is so often in adults. Infants do not fragment their presence, and they move through the different expressions of their presence as needs and drives arise. Fragmentation follows admonishment, violation or exploitation of children's particular ways of being.

CREATIVE EXPRESSION OF PRESENCE

Whilst creativity manifests itself in all expressions of being, it also has a life of its own. Babies, no less than adults, have an innate drive to express their uniqueness and individuality in creative ways as they get older. The means of doing that multiply — art, sports, dress, design, gardening, humour, drama, music, song, poetry, sculpture, pottery, mechanics, dance.

Even in the baby's early days of creativity you may get glimpses of what is to come from his or her athleticism or absorption in certain activities or colour preferences or inimitable responses to music or dance or mesmerisation by certain stimuli, such as television, animals, toys, sounds.

There is a deeper purpose to creativity, one that is more often than not knocked as the child gets older, and that is to live out our own unique lives.

Each child within a family finds distinct roles, interests, hobbies, identity (for example the academic, the sensitive one, the athlete, the wise one, the carer, the joker, the mechanic, the artistic one), food preferences, friends, dress preferences. Children have an innate determination to express their unique inner selves and, in spite of many blocks to this expression of self, they individualise in creative ways the very defences that are there to shield their real selves from further demeaning.

If only adults were in a place to appreciate the creativity used by children to express their difference within the social systems they live in. Difference is a manifestation of each person's sacred and unique origin, and its celebration would reduce much human misery.

SPIRITUAL EXPRESSION OF PRESENCE

In the beginning of their lives most babies (except those who experienced threat in the womb) are in the light of their unique presence and effectively are expressing:

- ☐ I am a unique and sacred individual (spiritual expression).
- ☐ My body is sacred and always right (physical expression).
- ☐ I am unconditionally lovable and I unconditionally love (emotional expression).
- ☐ I possess vast intelligence to make sense and order out of the people and worlds I encounter (intellectual expression).
- ☐ My behaviour always makes sense (behavioural expression).
- ☐ I am special, different, incomparable (social expression).
- ☐ I bring a uniquely creative presence to this world (creative presence).

When light meets light, light expands. When parents, adults and other children respond unconditionally to the ways in which infants express their unique selves, then they give babies an enlightened world to be in and to explore. Sadly, there is nobody who has had that experience of total acceptance, but the level of appreciation will determine how much light children retain and how much shadow they need to hide aspects of themselves that are a threat to others. Only when those who are the carers of infants are in the full light of their own presence are they in a position to affirm the light of infants' presence. Otherwise, to allow light to penetrate the darkness of fear, insecurity, terror, dependence and control of others would mean major risks to any level of protection that has been attained to date. For example, to move towards the light of independence from an overprotective parent could involve risking rejection and the parent plummeting into depression.

VOICES OF THE REAL SELF

Presence, real or shadowed, is concerned with the expression (real) or suppression (shadowed) of all essential aspects of self: physical, sexual, emotional, social, intellectual, creative, behavioural and spiritual. The expression or suppression of these several aspects of self can take myriad forms, which are unique to the individual person. The number, depth and breadth of these voices of the self are testament to the amazing power beyond measure that is present in each of us. These voices can be used to express your real self and also employed ingeniously to hide your real self, if threat is present. For example, language is a fascinating voice of the human being that can act to reveal or hide. An individual who is threatened by others can weave a colourful, endless tapestry of words when you are in their company and not allow you to get a word in edgeways. No matter how long you are with them, this continual verbal weave keeps flowing in order that your verbal voice is not allowed to threaten them. All the time they are hiding who they truly are behind the perpetual flow of words. Somehow this person has learned it is not safe just to be oneself in company. It is likely their early experiences were dominated by hypercriticism from one or both parents.

Body language is also a powerful indicator of whether people are being real or hidden. The body posture of the person who is true to self is sure, poised, energised, open and definite, in contrast to the person who hides his or her real self, with head down, shoulders hunched, low in energy, restless, uneasy. Similarly a person's dress or use of colour may provide indications of how they are in themselves.

Some examples of the voices of the psyche are given below. What is wondrous is that human beings keep developing new ways of self-expression. The technological revolution that is currently happening bears witness to this.

VOICES OF THE SELF

Words, thoughts, dreams, imagery, welfare feelings, emergency feelings, laughter, humour, delusions, illusions, hallucinations, projections, introjections, silence, inspiration, creativity, music, poetry, art, sculpture, song, prose, eye contact, tone of voice, body posture, body movement, behaviour, energy, touch, sexuality, dress, pain, sickness, diet, career, interests, hobbies, athleticism, dance, work, relationships, spirituality, violence, passivity, timidity, self-mutilation, home, slips of the tongue, colour, medication, metaphor.

Each of the voices can be used either to express clearly your own true self or to camouflage who you really are. In the latter case, the protective use of voices can provide clues as to what lies hidden behind the false façade that had to be created in order to survive.

PART TWO

PARTIAL ECLIPSE OF THE SELF

CHAPTER TWO
PEOPLE BLOCKS TO SELF-EXPRESSION

DARKNESS AS A METAPHOR FOR NEGLECT

Light is a wonderful symbol for the way most babies express their real presence. But early on, perils that shadow the light begin to emerge in relationships with other human beings whose own presence has been darkened in families and other social systems of community, school, classroom, workplace and country. These perils may threaten some or all of the infant's ways of expressing their true being.

It is not that parents or relatives or professional carers deliberately want to block the fullness of a child's presence, but when their own presence has been darkened, subconsciously they are not in a position to respond to the light of a child's presence.

The metaphors of darkness and shadow effectively express a state where a person's light becomes hidden. The metaphor of darkness to express a state of being is found in literature and in everyday speech; the mystics speak of 'the dark night of the soul', which is a powerful metaphor for being out of touch with the light of one's being. People who experience depression describe it as 'a black pit'; 'a dark emptiness'; 'a bottomless black hole'. I recall from my own experiences of depression the despair, the emptiness, the hopelessness and the darkness I felt at the dawn of each new day. I also remember a dark rage that at times, regrettably, threatened others. It is not that I wanted to hurt others, but my own hatred of myself prevented me from seeing and celebrating their unique presence. It is the darkness in ourselves — whether adults or children — that darkens the presence of others. Nonetheless, the effect is catastrophic and the cycle of darkness is repeated. For example, a parent who is terrified of expressing love can, in turn, instil the same defensive behaviour in his or her child.

BLOCKS TO THE EXPRESSION OF SELF

Blocks to being your real self begin in infancy and certainly accelerate and multiply as children get older. Parents, grandparents, childminders, playschool teachers, neighbours, school teachers and peers are all possible sources of threat to a child's real self. The frequency, intensity and endurance of these blocking behaviours are important determinants of the depth and extent of their effect.

Blocking behaviours are any behaviours — verbal or non-verbal — that demean, lessen and darken another person's presence. It is not just the actions that we experience directly that can threaten our presence, what happens between others can also be experienced as a threat to being real. For example, children who witness parents fighting with each other can learn to make themselves invisible in those times of crisis. In some cases the children of fighting parents become the rescuers and attempt to reduce the threat by becoming the go-between, and in doing so they, like the children who make themselves invisible, also diminish their own presence. Furthermore, where there is aggression and violence a child may either learn to do likewise with his or her own anger or learn that it is safer to suppress the feeling.

Typical blocking behaviours that children and adults alike may experience within relationships are:

- aggression
- blame
- comparisons
- competitiveness
- conditional love
- control
- cruelty
- cynicism
- denial
- dislike
- dismissiveness
- distance
- distrust
- dominance
- harshness
- hate
- hostile humour
- irritability
- jealousy
- manipulation
- meanness
- moodiness
- over-protection
- passivity
- physical violence
- punishment of failure
- 'put down' labels
- 'put up' labels
- rage
- ridicule
- rigidity
- sarcasm
- scolding
- sexual abuse
- success addiction
- threats
- unfair criticism

Threats to the real self occur not only through the presence of blocking behaviours but also through the absence of supportive behaviours. The greatest threat in many relationships is the lack of expression of love. Love is absolutely essential for human life; its non-expression lies at the heart of most human problems in living.

Typical supportive behaviours are:

- acceptance
- affection
- care
- celebration
- challenge
- compassion

- expression of emergency and welfare feelings
- fairness
- gentleness
- justice
- nurturance
- opportunities to experience your giftedness and unique potential
- physical care
- recognition
- respect
- responses to needs
- support
- understanding
- warmth

BLOCKS TO PHYSICAL PRESENCE

Our bodies are always right and ingeniously manifest our suppressed needs and the blocks that exist to the expression of our real self. Some parents see the body as basically 'bad' and attempt to correct its 'evil' by physical threats and other controlling responses such as:

- forced feeding
- forced toilet training
- irritability with crying
- frustration with soiling
- aggression at bedwetting
- rejection of physical contact
- medication for hyperactivity
- laxatives for constipation
- criticism of body shape
- insistence on 'looking right'

Blocks to your physical presence may be experienced through the verbal behaviour of others at all stages of life. The following examples may resonate with you.

As a child:

- □ 'Don't cry – it gives mammy a headache.'
- □ 'How is it you don't like what mammy has cooked for you?'
- □ 'You must eat your vegetables.'
- □ 'You're a bold child for wetting your bed.'
- □ 'Big boys don't wet their pants.'
- □ 'Sit quietly.'
- □ 'Your body is bad.'

As an adolescent:

- □ 'You're too fat.'
- □ 'A pity that you're not as good-looking as your sister.'
- □ 'Nobody would find you attractive.'
- □ 'You look like something the cat dragged in.'
- □ 'Your hair is a mess.'
- □ 'You don't care that how you look and dress affects me.'

As an adult:

- □ 'You're not going out dressed like that, are you?'
- □ 'Going thin on top, are we?'
- □ 'You think you're God's gift to women.'
- □ 'Without your sexy body you'd be nobody.'
- □ 'Putting on some weight, are we?'
- □ 'I hope we don't meet anybody – you look awful.'

BLOCKS TO EMOTIONAL PRESENCE

The primary need of human beings is to give and receive love. When the giving and receiving of love is present, an individual will experience a state of well-being. When the giving or receiving of love is blocked or, indeed, when love is neither shown nor given, a person will experience an emergency state. It is for this reason that welfare feelings (for example, love, joy, comfort, excitement, optimism, affection, enthusiasm, peacefulness, confidence) are indicative of a state of well-being, and emergency feelings (for example, fear, anger, sadness, jealousy, grief, resentment, horror, terror, frustration) express threats to security. All feelings are purposeful and need to be responded to positively. For many, responsiveness is not too difficult when it is welfare feelings that are being expressed (although individuals who have difficulty in sharing or receiving love can show punishing responses to such feelings). Emergency feelings tend to pose the greater threat to people and can give rise to mocking, dismissal, suppression, dilution, neutralisation (giving no recognition to the feeling) and punishment. Examples of blocking responses to the spontaneous expression of a person's emotional life are:

MOCKING

- □ 'Look at the weakling getting all upset.'
- □ 'Not angry again, are we?'
- □ 'You're a wimp, what are you?'
- □ 'You look like a wet rag.'
- □ 'Look at you with your big, red, angry face.'
- □ 'Big baby. Grow up and stop that crying.'

DISMISSAL

- □ 'I'm in no humour to listen to your woes.'
- □ 'For goodness sake will you stop getting upset about nothing.'

☐ 'Can't you see I'm busy? Come back later.'

SUPPRESSION

☐ 'It upsets me when you get angry.'
☐ 'I can't stand it when you start crying.'
☐ 'I'm sick of you feeling depressed.'

DILUTION

☐ 'What you're feeling is all in your head.'
☐ 'You will feel differently tomorrow.'
☐ 'You're going over the top with this.'

NEUTRALISATION

☐ 'So what's the problem?'
☐ 'Rationally, what you're feeling makes no sense.'
☐ 'We all get upset at times.'

PUNISHMENT

☐ 'Stop that or I'll spank you.'
☐ 'You're asking for it, going on like that.'
☐ 'No wonder I'm shouting at you; you're the one who started being angry.'

The intensity of the blocking response is expressed not only in the verbal reaction but also in the person's non-verbal responses – body posture, facial expression, tone of voice, speed of speech, nature of eye contact.

The examples above are concerned with blocks to the expression of emergency feelings, but it is important to realise that similar responses may be given to welfare feelings. For example, the expression of affection and

warmth can sometimes receive blocking responses, such as:

- ☐ 'Don't go all sloppy on me now.'
- ☐ 'I suspect you're looking for something from me.'
- ☐ 'Can't you see I'm busy right now?'
- ☐ 'You don't really feel like that.'
- ☐ 'You're only saying that to please me.'

Non-verbal reactions to the expression of welfare feelings can equally be perceived as threatening: tensing up, turning aside, resigned expression, pushing away, cynical facial expression.

All feelings need expression if individuals are to progress towards a realisation of self. Many people have learned not to express certain feelings, either because in earlier years the expression of feelings led to punishing responses, or because the significant adults in their life did not show certain feelings. In many cultures men have learned to cut themselves off from their heart and have difficulties in bringing forth feelings of love, affection, grief, sadness, fear, vulnerability or depression. Women too have learned to cut off from a side of their heart and can find it threatening to express feelings such as anger, power or determination.

It needs to be recognised that whilst women tend to be more emotionally literate than men, particularly with regard to expression of feelings, they are often poor at receiving those feelings from others. Similarly, whereas men are notoriously poor at the demonstration of both welfare and emergency feelings, compared to females, they are more open to accepting such feelings from others. When a mother is slow to receive welfare feelings, her children and others close to her will find it threatening to express those same feelings to her. The same holds true for the father — his non-expression of certain emotions will be picked up by his children and it will be threatening to them to express those feelings to him. I have worked with many people who are tormented by the fact that they have been unable to express love to their parents or other loved ones. The internal emotional life that mothers and fathers do not allow in themselves is projected onto those around him, and their children know intuitively not to threaten their parents by expression of feelings.

BLOCKS TO INTELLECTUAL PRESENCE

Every human being (except where there is brain damage due to congenital disease or trauma to the brain) is a genius. When you live with people who either doubt their own intelligence and have 'hang-ups' about their education, or who act superior to others because of a privileged educational background, then it is not safe to show your enormous intellectual potential; those who doubt themselves will put you down, and those whose identity is tied up with being intellectually superior will humiliate, dismiss or show you up.

There are multiple ways in which the wonderful ability of us all — young and old — to make sense and order of the world is blocked by the responses of others:

Impatience:
- 'How can it be taking so long for you to learn such a simple thing?'

Dismissiveness of your options, beliefs and value:
- 'How can you possibly think that?'

Criticism of your perceptions:
- 'That's not the way it is at all.'

Comparisons with another:
- ☐ 'Your cousin got far higher grades than you.'

Sarcasm:
- ☐ 'Well that turned out to be a really bright idea alright, didn't it?'

Ridicule of efforts to learn;
- ☐ 'A monkey could do better than that.'

Aggression in response to asserting your own views and perceptions:
- ☐ 'What the fuck do you know about anything?'

Punishment of failure:
- ☐ 'Failure is not tolerated here.'

Pressure to succeed:
- ☐ 'We want nothing less than A's.'

While responses such as those above may be intended to spur a person's intellectual development, they have, in fact, the opposite effect. No child or adult should have to put up with any darkening of their intellectual expression, but such an experience is a common phenomenon in the places in which we live, work, play, pray and learn.

BLOCKS TO BEHAVIOURAL PRESENCE

Behaviour is the wonderful means we have of exploring the inner world of self and the outer world of others and the universe. As seen, intellectually we possess all the power to assimilate and accommodate the world, but it is through our actions that we really get to grips with ourselves, others and the world. Fireside philosophising is no substitute for the actual experience of loving self, loving others and loving and exploring life. In their earliest days infants used their actions to get to know the confines of the cot and the mother's breast or feeding bottle. Within weeks the visible increase in behaviours is remarkable as infants begin to explore all that comes within their range. Natural curiosity, eagerness to learn and love of challenge are all there in those early days, but the blocks to the behavioural expression of these innate drives begin to appear quite early on and continue into childhood, adolescence and adulthood.

In any social system (family, classroom, school, community, workplace, peer group), each individual will find ingenious ways of behaving differently from the others in the system. In families it is commonly observed that each child's behavioural expression is completely different from the other brothers and sisters. When difference is affirmed and lauded by parents, teachers, leaders and managers, it gives people the fertile ground to thrive as the unique and creative individuals they truly are. Sadly, the promotion of sameness and conformity are far more common experiences than affirmation of difference. In the workplace a sense of anonymity is a frequently voiced complaint of employees. In order that behavioural expression of self prospers, we need encouragement, support, praise, enthusiasm, understanding, patience, excitement, fun and healthy humour. But what most children and adults experience are blocks to expression of the following kinds:

☐ emphasis on getting things right
☐ criticism and/or physical punishment of failure
☐ impatience with level of effort
☐ intolerance of doing nothing
☐ non-recognition of behavioural expressions
☐ demands to do things the same way as others

- lack of opportunities to explore
- curtailment of creativity
- disappointment with results of efforts
- 'yes but' response to attainments
- over-rewarding of success
- boasting about achievements
- threatening responses when challenges are taken up
- forcing individuals to do things that do not inspire them
- unfair and unrealistic expectations
- over-burdening with responsibilities
- not recognising the individuality in people's behavioural expression
- comparing achievements with those of others
- only seeing what has not been done
- compelling individuals to carry out activities that they are not socially or emotionally ready to do

Certainly, the absence of praise and recognition is a serious blow to efforts to attain knowledge and skills. Demands for conformity to the ways of others and lack of or curtailment of opportunities to explore your giftedness and unlimited potential are familiar limits that people encounter to behavioural expression. The 'yes but' response leads to great insecurity, because no matter how intense and fruitful your efforts have been, there is always something you have missed, and this is over-emphasised to the detriment of what you have attained. Many people believe that great joy and rewarding of success is a means to increasing behavioural exploration, but this is a projection of their own need to be seen as successful and it can either seriously block exploration or limit it to the area of the 'enforced' behaviour. It also results in behaviour becoming performance-driven rather than challenging.

People need to be encouraged, particularly in those behaviours which inspire them and which don't go against their own grain. Avoidance of and not taking up certain challenges are frequently confused. Avoidance results from fear, whereas not having interest in particular challenges may either be because the challenge is uninspiring, or because it will not serve the purpose of establishing a distinct identity.

Finally, responsibilities and expectations need to be in keeping with a person's age, gender, social circumstances and present level of attainment. An example is the situation where some children are given adult responsibilities or some adults are only given childish responsibilities.

BLOCKS TO SOCIAL PRESENCE

The social presence of every human being is a unique phenomenon and each child or adult has the right to have their specialness acknowledged. There is no greater boost to a child or an adult than to let them know warmly and genuinely: 'You are one of a kind and special.' A mother who had recognised how conditional she had been with her four-year-old son told him one day, 'You are very special to me.' To her astonishment he replied, 'And to think that I don't have to do anything for that!' Make no mistake about it: infants and children know full well the difference between unconditional and conditional acceptance.

The social presence of human beings – children and adults – can be violated in many ways:

- ignoring their presence or absence
- not addressing them by their preferred title
- giving them nicknames

- □ turning away from them
- □ being irritable and tetchy with them
- □ being dismissive
- □ leaving them isolated
- □ ostracising them
- □ gossiping about them
- □ making snide comments about them
- □ showing non-verbal disdain of their presence
- □ excluding them from conversation
- □ criticising them publicly
- □ acting superior
- □ not being hospitable towards them
- □ making sarcastic comments
- □ having double social standards
- □ putting pressure on them to conform

BLOCKS TO SEXUAL EXPRESSION

In the same way that the body of every person is sacred, so too is its sexual expression. Free sexual expression of self suffers major blows not only from other individuals but from the cultures we inhabit. The last decade has seen revelation upon revelation of violations of the sexual integrity of children and women in homes, schools, churches, communities, institutions of care and workplaces. Gradually too it is becoming clear that the sexual integrity of boys and men has also been frequently violated. The pervasiveness of the sexual pornography industry, particularly child pornography, as well as sado-masochism, bestiality and other insults to sacredness, bear witness to continued blocks to mature sexual expression and exploration. Difference in sexual expression (homosexuality, transexuality, transvestism) are still the subject of ridicule, hostile humour, aggression, violence and sometimes murder.

Infants' exploration and enjoyment of their erogenous zones is not usually well received by the adults who care for them. Many adults get embarrassed, horrified or aggressive when babies touch themselves and others sexually. Some parents react harshly when a young child self-stimulates; sadly this reaction can have devastating effects on the young person's sexual maturation. These reactions are a product of adults' discomfort with and rejection or repression of their own sexuality. There is no question that children need to be guided into a socially acceptable way of being sexual and to be helped to see the dangers of being sexually exploited by others. But guidance is a very different process to suppression or repression of sexual development. Rejection or repression often results in our 'erogenous' zones being experienced as our 'erroneous' zones.

Blocks to a child's sexual expression can be physical, verbal and non-verbal:

PHYSICAL

- □ inappropriate touching and holding of children
- □ kissing children in a sexual way
- □ sexualising children before their time
- □ exposing children to sexual materials (internet, video, magazines)
- □ sexually exposing self
- □ dressing children in a sexually provocative way
- □ getting children to touch an adult's or other child's erogenous zones
- □ attempting or accomplishing vaginal, anal or oral intercourse

INDIRECT PHYSICAL ACTIONS

- being naked and sexually aroused around children
- leaving sexually explicit materials about the place
- watching pornographic videos in the presence of children
- self-stimulating in the presence of children
- having sexual intercourse in front of children

VERBAL

- talking explicitly on sexual matters
- verbally inviting children to touch themselves or another
- relating stories of sexual exploits
- requesting children to show their 'privates'
- asking children to 'kiss me just there'
- inviting children 'to be the doctor'

As with children, blocks to an adult's sexual expression can be directly or indirectly physical or verbal:

DIRECTLY PHYSICAL

- inappropriate sexual gesturing
- uninvited showing of pornography
- uninvited sexual exposure
- unsolicited sexual touching
- forced sexual contact

INDIRECTLY PHYSICAL

- being stripped by another's eyes
- ogling
- watching pornographic videos without consideration of other people present
- self-stimulating in presence of a reluctant other

VERBAL

- ☐ verbal sexual harassment
- ☐ conversation that portrays the person as a sexual object
- ☐ uninvited voicing of sexual exploits
- ☐ sexual jokes that debase the person and sexuality
- ☐ vulgar remarks of a sexual nature

BLOCKS TO CREATIVE PRESENCE

Creativity is the unique giftedness that each person has to express his or her presence, to acknowledge the presence of others and to explore the world. In spite of pressures to conform and non-support or ridiculing of difference, it is amazing that children will always manage to create a distinct, if protective, identity. If children and adults had their innate difference and individuality celebrated and nourished so that they did not have to resort to protection, then how much more powerful would be their presence and productivity.

But difference is not highly valued, whilst conforming, 'playing the game', being 'one of the lads', being 'a yes person' are more highly rewarded. The construction of creativity through social demands is well illustrated in the everyday example of dress code. I remember arriving on a warm summer morning to give a lecture to business people on a day's cruise on a car ferry and being astonished that all the men wore ties and both men and women were dressed in formal suits. They were following the convention of business attire rather than dressing in a manner comfortable for them and suitable to the particular occasion.

The blocking of creativity can happen in a myriad of ways:

- ☐ comparison with others

- ☐ criticism
- ☐ cynicism
- ☐ disdain
- ☐ hostile humour
- ☐ judgment
- ☐ mockery
- ☐ ridicule
- ☐ sarcasm

The vastness of creativity can be greatly diminished when there is over-emphasis on successful creation and when a person's worth is made conditional on their creative output. As a result, people may either hide their talents under a bushel for fear of failure or become addicted to success. People who are addicted to success put immense pressure on themselves (and others) to maintain impossible standards. These individuals can be a high suicide risk, particularly at the point where they feel they have reached the zenith of their creativity.

Creativity is best enjoyed for its intrinsic value, not for extrinsic rewards.

BLOCKS TO SPIRITUAL PRESENCE

Any blow — physical, emotional, behavioural, intellectual, sexual, social — is a block to a person's sacred and spiritual presence. Each human being is a remarkable phenomenon, and honouring of this is vital to his or her spirituality. The experience of your spiritual presence is not truly possible until you have found love of self and love of others. Two of the greatest spiritual teachers echo this belief. Buddha declared that you can travel the whole world and find nobody more deserving of love than yourself. Christ made it very clear that the love of self is the foundation of the love of your neighbour and the transcendence to a love of God.

Ironically, one of the most powerful blocks to spirituality has been institutionalised religion. In the Catholic religion, for example, the very thing for which Christ castigated the Pharisees: 'You make it as if man was made for law, not the law for man', the Church repeated. Christ went on to say that 'there is only one law, 'that you love God with all your heart, and your neighbour *as yourself*'. Dogma, moralising and judgment have been and still are integral to many religions. The notion too that people basically are flawed and there are the 'chosen few' still exists. Hierarchical structures, superiority and patriarchy are still present in many churches. All of these are blocks to spirituality.

Any blow to the self-worth of the individual is a block to spirituality, but in addition there are certain behaviours that directly block the experience of our spiritual presence:

- □ lack of opportunities to explore our spiritual nature
- □ punishment of spiritual practices
- □ ridicule of spiritual beliefs and actions
- □ viewpoint that sees the person as basically 'evil', 'sinful', or 'flawed'
- □ absence of celebration and affirmation of the sacredness of the person
- □ religions that are dogmatic, controlling and patriarchal
- □ absence of role models of spirituality

From my own experiences over the years, from an early time of spiritual experiences, to spending seven years in a Catholic monastery, and then years of believing in nothing and being dangerously cynical, to recent years of touching back into a sense of something greater and enduring in myself, one of the lessons I have learned is that you cannot think yourself into spirituality. Spirituality is both a heart and mind phenomenon, and it is through opening up our hearts and minds to our true nature that glimpses of our spiritual nature arises.

CHAPTER THREE
CULTURES THAT DARKEN HUMAN PRESENCE

NATURE OF CULTURE

There are several different cultural levels. The first culture is the culture within each person. The second culture encountered is the mother's womb, then the family, the community, the school, the church, the county, the country, the continent and the world. Within a particular culture there may be sub-cultures; for example, a community culture can have ghetto areas or a marginalised group, or, in a school, one classroom can be a distinct sub-culture and not reflect the ethos of the wider school culture. All cultures are inter-connected, even when there is conflict either within or between the different cultures.

The amazing aspect of a culture is that even though it is extremely difficult to define how it comes about or what it is, you sense its presence and know its advantages and limitations. When a culture is positive, powerful and creative, possibilities abound for all members. The healthy culture recognises the needs of each member to express individuality and to live out life in creative and unique ways; it also recognises the influence of group presence and creates structures that ensure care for all and the need for collective responsibility. This culture also emphasises the inter-connectedness of all its members and the necessity of co-operation and shared responsibility to effect inner personal and outer social harmony. The more a culture is in touch with the rights and needs of the individual and the group, the greater the level of cultural intimacy. The contrary is also true. When it elicits either an over-belonging or an under-belonging, then its members can become demoralised, demeaned, marginalised and lessened. An over-belonging culture is where there is an over-dominating involvement by the social system in people's lives that severely restrains individuality, creativity and personal initiative. Indeed such a culture promotes helplessness in its members. An under-belonging culture is where too much is demanded, and dominance, coercion and rigidity are the forces used to ensure conformity. This kind of culture leads to dependence and control by others. Far from appraising radical thought, individuality, assertiveness and non-conformity, in this kind of culture any falling short of cultural demands may be dealt with harshly.

Regrettably there are even darker cultures than the two described above, where total neglect, exploitation and downright cruelty exists. Violence, torture, aggression, harassment or a total lack of physical, emotional and social care of members are part and parcel of such cultures. Military regimes, fundamentalist religions, rigid and punishing educational systems, workplaces where members are treated like cogs in a wheel, or families that are highly neglectful of the welfare of their members are examples of such cultures.

There is another type of culture which, even though in appearance it may be kind, caring and responsive to needs, on closer examination reveals an unrelenting demand for sameness and the exclusion of outsiders. This culture is characteristic of fundamentalist groups, 'cult' organisations and symbiotic families.

Where cultural harmony exists, what is apparent is what really is; where disharmony prevails, what is apparent is not what it is all about. In the latter case, similar to a 'black economy' that exists in a society where the rich get richer and the poor poorer, a 'black sub-culture' develops and, depending on the level of disharmony in the visible culture, this secret culture can sometimes be more powerful than the one you see. Such a phenomenon is visible in the revelations of sexual and physical violations perpetrated by a clergy whose sexual and emotional needs were not honoured by their Church.

MAJOR CULTURAL FORCES WE EXPERIENCE

It is both an individual and cultural responsibility that each person be enabled to be real and to affirm the unique and sacred person of others. Over many years of helping individuals, couples and employees, their stories indicated that the cultures they were members of were not noted for acknowledging, celebrating or promoting the individuality of their members. On the contrary, the more common experiences were dismissal, double-standards, demands for conformity, non-listening, dominance, control, passivity, physical neglect, sexual harassment, gender inequity, aggression, superiority.

The cultures most spoken about by persons who have come for help are family, school, church and workplace. I am certainly aware of the effects of some political and govern-mental social agencies on people's lives, but not to the same extent as those mentioned by clients. Given that this book is more geared towards individuals who have been adversely affected by family, school, church and work organisation, it is my intention to focus on these four cultures. In no way does this imply that political and social cultures do not need to reflect on their practices.

These different influences come together to form the overall culture and can be extremely powerful either in blocking or supporting the emergence of the real self. Cultural forces do not operate independently of each other but, like a spider's web, are enmeshed so that where there are dark influences, they criss-cross in a bi-directional way; this applies also to good influences. For example, the family culture is tremendously influenced by the wider culture, and by conforming to the wider culture's restraining or progressive forces, it maintains and reinforces their existence. An instance of a restraining situation is where, in a religious culture that is demanding and terror-inducing, the same dynamic can be repeated in the family, which too rejects an individual family member who does not conform to the religious demands.

Oppressive political systems, educational systems that are performance and academic driven, economies that demand the mass of people 'tighten their belts' while a minority are 'expanding their belts', work cultures that are exploitative and uncaring, medical practices that are prescriptive and purely biological in perspective, religions that control and judge, psychiatric approaches that label, drug and suppress the human spirit, psychological systems that presumptuously believe they know the answers to an individual's or family's problems, and social agencies that judge, marginalise, label and discriminate — all these influence the dynamic of the family and how individuals respond to each other. For example, the adolescent girl who is labelled schizophrenic is no longer seen as a precious member of the family and is given over to the 'care' of a psychiatric system; the young man who refuses to look for employment becomes an embarrassment and tends to be treated as a second-class citizen by social agencies, the drop-out from school is hidden or denigrated by the family and viewed as a failure by the educational system; the successful student or careerist is lauded above others and often is exploited in the workplace; the sick person is seen as weak or a failure and a burden on health services; the non-believer in religion is castigated; and the person who is apolitical is judged as being irresponsible. When the family fails to confront such influences, it is extremely difficult for the individual to 'take on the world of darkness'.

FAMILY CULTURES THAT DARKEN HUMAN PRESENCE

Our first and very powerful experience of culture is within the family, and it is the family which is the most important determinant of the level of light and shadow shown by each individual. Values, attitudes, traditions, assumptions and norms differ from family to family, but are all profoundly influenced by the wider cultures of church, community, school, workplace and country. Stereotypical roles for men and women and mothers and fathers still predominate and limit individuals of both genders. To a great extent, at least in Western cultures, women have freed themselves of being tied to kitchen, bedroom and church, but they still carry 90 per cent of the responsibility for home-making and child-rearing. Many men still believe that career takes precedence over their family and partner, and still hold to the 'breadwinner' role.

Males are still expected to 'put a brave face' on their troubles and not cry, admit regret, be vulnerable or show weakness. Many men believe they can control through aggression. In Europe and America at least 25 per cent of women still experience violence at the hands of their male partners.

However, growing numbers of men are victim to female assaults.

The upbringing of boys and girls remains influenced by the misguided attitude that 'boys will be boys', and so should be tough, and 'girls will be girls', and so should be caring, nurturing and selfless. Addiction to caring is still strong among women, whilst addiction to work is common among men.

Family attitudes to sexuality, though less rigid than in the past, still result in sex being a taboo subject.

Globalisation and pluralism have had a profound influence on our culture in the last two decades and have broken the stranglehold that the Church has had over family, educational, social, sexual and political life. The influence of pluralism on family culture is evident in more flexible attitudes towards parenting, discipline, relationships, education, career development, spirituality and religion.

While positive changes are evident, nonetheless there are still many aspects of family culture that lessen the presence of its members. Probably the most important issue is that individuals who are themselves in shadow are allowed to take on the most difficulty responsibility of all — parenting — without any preparation, training or reflection on their own sense of self. It seems such a nonsense that the family social system, which is at the heart of the wider culture, is not taken more seriously. Lip service is given to the importance of the family by governments, but is not reflected in action.

A further issue is that the wider culture has not taken on board sufficiently the rapid rise in single parents, divorce, desertion, same-sex parents, surrogate parents and working parents. We have little idea yet of the influences of some of these changes on children's development. It is known that divorce and separation *per se* do not significantly limit children's progress, but conflict, whether among divorced or separated parents or in intact unhappy marriages, has major influences on children's security. A worrying social trend is the phenomenon of the fatherless family; it is still the case that following divorce or separation 90 per cent of women are left holding the babies, and neither individuals nor social agencies are doing anything to confront this development.

The demise of the extended family is frequently lamented, but I am not convinced that the loss is a great one. Certainly the extended family that supported and encouraged the individuality, difference, freedom and independence of young people should be sorely missed. However, the more common dark reality is the extended family that pushes for conformity among its members and maintains at all costs the illusion that 'all families are happy families'.

Families come in all shapes, sizes and structures; what counts is the nature of the attitudes and actions that drive the daily life of the family.

CHARACTERISTICS OF FAMILIES THAT DARKEN MEMBERS' PRESENCE

- □ belief in and use of physical punishment
- □ physical/emotional violation of children by parents
- □ violent/verbal bullying among siblings
- □ couple conflict
- □ dominance and control
- □ double standards
- □ lack of emotion
- □ hierarchical family structure
- □ interference/intrusion by parents-in-law
- □ lack of love
- □ over-protection/under-protection

- □ over-emphasis on religion
- □ addiction problem in parent(s)
- □ acute/chronic emotional distress in parent(s)
- □ long-term physical illness or disablement in a parent
- □ sexual problems in a parent
- □ poverty
- □ stereotyping of males and females
- □ symbiosis (no individuality permitted)
- □ symptoms of insecurity ignored
- □ conflictual three-generation family

The over-protective or over-involved parent elicits in children such survival responses as neediness, dependence, powerlessness, helplessness and relinquishment of the right to live one's own life. Similarly, the under-protective or under-involved family dynamic fails to inspire its members or celebrate their individual presence, thereby leading to apathy and a sense of 'what's the point of it all'. In the dominant and controlling family, rule is maintained through cajoling, criticism, punishment and creating a fearful atmosphere. The members of this family may achieve highly, but instead of being driven by challenge and love of life, they are driven by fear of not being good enough. The insecurity of not being loved for themselves blocks their path through life.

The symbiotic family allows no individuality; the family takes over the individual and moves and directs its life as one entity. Sameness, rigid conformity and isolation from outside cultures are typical of this extremely shadowed family.

There are emotionless families where all feelings are repressed and the prime needs to love and be loved and to express one's interior emotional world are totally blocked. The loveless family permits neither the expression of emergency feelings (for example, fear, anger, sadness, upset) nor the showing of welfare feelings (for example, love, joy, excitement, enthusiasm). Whilst physical, educational and career development may be nurtured, there is a powerful threat to showing or asking for love.

It is important to see that the parents who are the architects of dark family cultures are themselves personally in great shadow, and their protections against experiences of being demeaned and lessened in this world are subtle, complex and extensive. Their intention is not to block the presence of other family members, but to dull the pain of their own sense of invisibility.

EDUCATIONAL CULTURES THAT DARKEN HUMAN PRESENCE

Many school cultures demean and lessen the presence not only of students but of teachers. Low staff morale, high levels of absenteeism, high rates of psychosomatic illness, early retirement on grounds of illness and stress, burnout and 'rustout' (apathy) are the common fallout responses to school cultures that are not responsive to the unique presence, rights and needs of all their members. The focus of schools has traditionally been on a narrow interpretation of education, and, more recently, on successful achievement in what are seen as life-determining state examinations. The academic emphasis places great pressure on both teachers and students. Teachers experience demands from management, from parents and from students themselves. Due to the common confusion of knowledge with intelligence and the bias towards academic learning, the school culture tends to label students as 'dull', 'weak', 'slow', 'average', 'bright', 'brilliant'. All these labels have a profound effect on children's view of themselves and many of them carry these blocking effects from their childhood to their graves. You may believe the students labelled 'brilliant', 'clever', or 'genius' are the fortunate ones, but these labels put great pressure on these students to maintain high performance levels for the rest of their lives. The dark force of always having to 'be the clever one' can cause as much havoc to being real as the dark force of the label of 'the slow one'. These persons who strive for perfection have a higher risk of suicide than those who adopt the protection of being 'drop-outs'.

A school culture that does not celebrate the uniqueness, sacredness, individuality and difference of all its members seriously blocks the emergence of all that is wonderful and powerful in us as human beings. An educational philosophy that is not holistic in nature and does not encompass concern for the emotional, social, physical, sexual, social, educational, intellectual, creative and spiritual development of students acts as a dark force in the lives of those exposed to it.

Discipline problems in school have become a major issue. If the school is to meet its obligation to protect its members' rights to physical, emotional, social, intellectual and sexual safety, then it has to address lapses of discipline firmly and respectfully; to do otherwise would be to block seriously the presence of all concerned. Bullying to some degree or other occurs in all schools, not just among students, but between teachers and students, teachers and teachers, parents and teachers, management and teachers. The consequences of bullying can be loss of a sense of self-worth, as well as passive reactions of fear, withdrawal, depression or suicide, or counter-aggressive reactions of rage, violence, sabotage or even murder. One can imagine the dark view of society children hold when adults or other children are allowed to bully them without fear of redress. And those children who bully others without being hindered — what do they think of us?

Large class sizes can mean that individual children do not get sufficient opportunity to explore their giftedness and vast potential, and teachers do not have the chance to exercise fully their teaching skills. Teachers can find that far too much time is spent dealing with large numbers, discipline problems, poor motivation and isolation. The lack of or token back-up psychological and social services adds to their frustration. Governments for far too long have burdened teachers with responsibilities that are outside their field of expertise; teachers are often called upon to be clinical psychologists, educational psychologists, family therapists, counsellors, nurses or spiritual directors. The teaching profession needs to hold to the boundaries of its field of expertise and not be controlled by the wider systems of government and families. When this happens the resources needed to tackle many of the problems in classrooms and schools may begin to emerge.

The ethos of a school can range from an under-belonging at one extreme to over-belonging at the other extreme. In either case students and teachers alike can feel demeaned, lessened and controlled. The more common under-belonging ethos puts great emphasis on academic attainment and rigid discipline, and shows little real interest in the emotional, social, creative and spiritual worlds of its members. Examination results and order in the classroom come before people. Those who conform are lauded, whilst those who fall short can very definitely be punished and marginalised. The over-belonging school tends to do too much for students, shows low expectations, does not offer challenges, does not show belief in children's amazing intellectual potential and giftedness and, generally speaking, promotes helplessness. Under-belonging may be seen as expecting too much from the 'head', whereas over-belonging operates too much from the heart. An effective ethos reaches out to students and teachers with both mind and heart.

It is by the actions of a cultural system, and the frequency, intensity and duration of those actions, that you can best evaluate the extent of its darkening influence.

CHARACTERISTICS OF A DARK SCHOOL CULTURE

- □ academic standards take precedence over valuing and caring of teachers
- □ bias towards academic subjects
- □ confusion of intelligence with knowledge
- □ double standards for teachers and students
- □ ineffective leadership
- □ labelling students as 'weak', 'slow', 'bright', 'brilliant'
- □ limited resources for students (and teachers) to explore their unique vast potential and giftedness
- □ little or inconsistent involvement of parents
- □ exclusion of significant members (parents, teachers, students) from decisions on school policies
- □ learning takes precedence over valuing students
- □ low level of staff commitment
- □ lack of or inadequate back-up service to deal with bullying
- □ lack of or inadequate discipline system
- □ not person nor family friendly
- □ over-rewarding of success
- □ poor staff morale
- □ punishment of failure
- □ lack of or inadequate specialised help for students who need it
- □ teachers left isolated in classrooms

□ teachers in need of professional help being allowed to continue to teach and not being requested to seek help
□ teaching style that is aggressive, passive or passive-aggressive
□ undisciplined behaviour on the part of teachers or students being allowed to go unchallenged

Once a young mother approached me at the end of a lecture and told me of her six-year-old daughter who complained of stomach pains, nausea and headaches every morning before going to school. During her first year in school she had had no such complaints; indeed she was excited and looked forward to school each day. Her mother quickly explained that her experiences in her first year could be attributed to the fact that 'she had a lovely teacher last year'. This begged the question: 'What kind of teacher has she got this year'? The mother replied: 'Well she has a reputation for being very critical and cross and she shouts at the children'. When I asked her what was she going to do about the fact that her child was 'sick with fear' going into the teacher's classroom she replied, 'There is little I can do; many parents have complained but nothing changes'. She then added 'but she'll have a lovely teacher next year'. My fear was that her child would be totally turned off school by the time next year came around, and no 'nice teacher' would be able to convince her that school was a safe place. I advised the mother to go to see the Principal of the school and to convey her intention that she would not allow her child to attend school until the matter was resolved, and if no resolution was forthcoming, that she intended to find a healthier school environment for her child. I also suggested she inform the Department of Education on the matter. These latter suggestions were not meant to threaten the teacher's position, but the emotional difficulties of any individual cannot be allowed to darken the presence of others. In truth, this teacher needed some intervention as much as the child, and it was a major failure on the school's part not to have addressed the issues of both involved.

RELIGIOUS CULTURES THAT DARKEN HUMAN PRESENCE

The major religions have been notoriously patriarchal, with the consequence that the presence of women has been particularly darkened. In Christianity the concept of the person as basically evil and flawed has greatly blocked the emergence of what is true and sacred in each human being. Fear was and still is a weapon that the Church used to control its congregation. Feelings of unworthiness, scrupulosity, terror of living and dying were some of the results of such dominance.

The notion too that one earned worthiness or that only 'the chosen few' would be saved was highly discriminating. Enforced celibacy for priests and nuns and 'natural' contraception for couples caused much hardship to many members. Anti-divorce and anti-sex attitudes trapped many individuals in sexless, loveless and sometimes violent marriages.

Hierarchical power structures led to positions of superiority and inferiority. The belief too that some people were 'called' to the priesthood, sisterhood or brotherhood implied that some people were more sacred than others — surely the ultimate sacrilege! Ironically, many individuals in the 'call' professions were exploited by the Church.

Religious control of educational systems not only limited curriculum development, but discriminated against those who were not 'members of the flock'. Teachers, students and parents who were homosexual in orientation, or who were non-believers or who were having 'illicit' relationships had to hide their true selves and lived in fear of being 'found out' or 'outed'.

The religious notions of sin, confession and forgiveness are judgmental and controlling in nature and are strongly guilt-inducing. Mutual responsibility between members of any culture is central to its survival. However, labelling, judging, marginalising, incarcerating, ostracising and threatening behaviours only create shadow around the goodness and compassion that is in the heart of every human being.

There are some individuals within the Churches who are striving to bring forth the spirituality and wisdom of Christ, but the age-old structures are sunk deep into the ground and cast long shadows.

A religious culture needs to be worthy of your dignity and unique sacredness; when it is not then both individual members and the Church itself have difficult questions to ask themselves.

CHARACTERISTICS OF DARK RELIGIOUS CULTURES

- □ controlling
- □ demanding rigid conformity
- □ discriminating (gender, sexual orientation)
- □ being dogmatic
- □ having double standards
- □ having hierarchical power structures
- □ being judgmental
- □ lacking compassion
- □ law-giving (rather than love-giving)

- being materialistic
- being moralistic
- being non-reflective
- being patriarchal
- seeing human beings as fundamentally 'bad' or flawed

WORK CULTURES THAT DARKEN HUMAN PRESENCE

Work culture is similar to other cultures in the sense that its foundation lies in traditions, values and shared basic assumptions, but it is more narrowly focused than other cultures.

Traditionally work cultures have not been person, couple or family friendly. Many workers complain of anonymity in the workplace, whilst others feel diminished, demeaned and humiliated. Bullying is still characteristic of most management and murder is the most common cause of death in the workplace in America. Recent research in Britain indicates that 90 per cent of workers experience some form of bullying.

Some work cultures are militaristic in approach, running a tight outfit with emphasis on control of workers and high productivity. The 'team' culture is a common one, where rewards are given for being a good team player, and poor performance leads to being firmly sidelined. Winning at all costs and playing the game is what matters. Individuality, difference and non-conformity are viewed as major threats and can lead to being marginalised or excluded. There are some work cultures that are the 'big happy family' dynamic, but this 'work family' is expected to take precedence over personal development, family and couple relationships. Individuality is not affirmed, but conformity is strongly endorsed.

The militaristic, athletic and 'happy family' type work cultures are all conditional in their relationships with workers: once you 'toe the line' your loyalty will reap you conditional regard and respect, promotion and financial rewards. However, none of these three cultures promotes personal independence, initiative and creativity, and they are not person or family friendly.

There are far more seriously neglectful work organisations than those mentioned above. These can be either mechanistic (treat workers like machines) or animalistic (treat workers like animals). Within these work places there is absolutely no respect for person, family or couples, and exploitation is the order of the day. Human endeavour is not valued. Verbal and physical threats rule the workers, and any attempt to confront injustice is dealt with harshly. Such dark workplaces are characteristic of some Third World countries, but in my clinical practice I have been told stories of considerable demeaning of employees within so-called reputable companies or in family-run businesses.

Some of the many aspects of work cultures that are blocks to the manifestation of an employee's, or an employer's, real self are listed below:

CHARACTERISTICS OF DARK WORK CULTURES

- passing people over for promotion
- boring, repetitive work
- bullying
- double standards for management and rank and file workers
- inequality
- lack of appreciation

- unjust wages for labour
- lack of back-up system to deal with neglect of workers
- lack of consultation or changes in working conditions or job description
- lack of consideration of worker's life outside work
- lack of respectful communication
- lack of opportunities to develop skills, exercise responsibility and show vast potential
- long working hours
- management style that is aggressive or passive or passive-aggressive
- no overtime pay
- not person, couple or family friendly
- poor physical working conditions
- purely 'profit' focused
- sexual harassment
- unfair dismissal

In examining the blocks to your worth in the workplace, the frequency, intensity and endurance of these lessening forces need to be part of your decision to take whatever actions are needed to nurture your sense of dignity and worthiness.

CHAPTER FOUR
HIDING YOUR REAL SELF

IN DEFENCE OF THE LIGHT

The sophisticated and terrifying physical weapons that nations have developed to defend their geographical boundaries and their political, social and religious cultures are well known and accepted as legitimate means of protection. At the individual level, people put alarm systems in their homes, cars and business places, they have 'watch' dogs and carry weapons such as guns, knives, coshes and other protective devices. People put their valuables in 'safe' places and employ security guards and up-to-date security devices to guard their possessions. Nobody questions the wisdom of these practices, but somehow when it comes to guarding your sacred self from threats to your unique expression, less acceptance and understanding is shown. This response is a defence against individuals acknowledging their own dark forces and taking on the responsibility to free themselves of the shackles of a persona that was developed to please the outer world. Inevitably such a forward step stirs up insecurity in others and thereby increases the blocks to being your true self. Until the time is right, you will wisely stay in the shadow of the amazing emotional, social, sexual, intellectual and behavioural strategies you employ in response to attacks on your real self.

ONCE BITTEN, TWICE SHY

A young woman was brought to see me by her parents because she was extremely timid, refused to go outdoors, had no friends, lacked confidence and had no ambition. She was one of the shyest young persons I had ever come across. Her head was down and turned sideways, she made no eye contact, her posture was bent forward and her voice was extremely low. She apologised constantly for being there, and any question she posed was followed by 'I shouldn't have asked that, should I?' At one stage I asked her if she had heard of the expression 'once bitten, twice shy', to which she answered 'yes'. I then asked her how many times did she reckon she had been bitten? She answered spontaneously 'seven, eight hundred times'. It emerged that not only had she been seriously intimidated by a domineering and controlling mother, but she had also endured considerable bullying from her peers during her school years. Her father was of little support because of his own passivity and his failure to confront his wife on her difficult behaviour. I pointed out to the young woman how ingenious she was in developing the protections of extreme shyness and avoidance of contact. The more frequent, enduring and intense the blocking behaviours to the expression of your true self, the greater the level of protection needed, and this young person had wisely learned to hide her real self from a world of people and social systems that had not affirmed her presence. She was no weakling but a tower of strength in the face of what was a constant onslaught on her true self.

When you analyse this young woman's defensive behaviours, it is clear that her armamentarium for guarding her real self included behavioural, emotional, social, physical and intellectual weapons:

☐ *Behavioural:* avoidance of risk-taking, lack of ambition, blaming of others, staying in her room, not mixing with others in school.

- □ *Physical:* no eye contact, bent body posture, lowered head, frequent infections.
- □ *Intellectual:* labelling of herself as 'weak', comparing herself with others who were getting on with life, imagining herself as 'ugly, unlovable and pathetic'.
- □ *Social:* withdrawal from all contact with people and the outside world.
- □ *Emotional:* shy, depressed, terrified, timid, hurt, covertly hostile to others.

It is important to see that each of the above responses is clever and inventive, designed to counter the attacks on self that she experienced. When her need for protection is not understood by those around her, it can lead to responses that are judgmental, derisory, hostile and mocking, and thereby lead to an increase in the victim's protective strategies. When examined, the resourcefulness of her protective devices begins to be seen as educational and inspiring.

BEHAVIOURAL PROTECTION

- □ *no risk-taking* means no failure, and no failure means no ridicule.
- □ *lack of ambition* eliminates expectations, and no expectations mean no failure, no criticism.
- □ *blaming of others* — by blaming parents, peers and teachers for her 'sorry state', she rules out having to look to herself as the primary source of her protections.
- □ *staying in her room* — no contact, no hurt.
- □ *not mixing with others in school* — isolation, no violation.

PHYSICAL PROTECTION

- □ *no eye contact* means no connection, and no connection means no possibilities of hurt.

☐ *bent body posture* prompts sympathy and a 'tip-toeing' response, thereby reducing expectations.

☐ *lowered head, turned sideways* elicits sympathy and few expectations; fewer expectations equal fewer possibilities of dissatisfaction on the part of parents, peers and teachers.

INTELLECTUAL PROTECTION

☐ *labelling herself* as 'weak' invites a sympathetic response and has the effect of people asking less of her.

☐ *comparison with others* — she does not have to look at herself and it keeps the focus on others so that no challenge is required.

☐ *limited image of self* — in seeing herself as ugly, unlovable and pathetic she justifies her avoidance behaviours and controls others by generating sympathetic responses.

SOCIAL PROTECTION

☐ *social phobia* — out of sight equals out of hurt.

EMOTIONAL PROTECTION

☐ *emotional vulnerability* is cleverly designed to reduce, minimise or eliminate threats to being real, as people tend to back off and not make demands.

COUNTERING BLOCKS TO EXPRESSION OF YOUR REAL SELF

Blocks to the expression of your real self arise from many sources. The frequency, intensity and endurance of these blocks will determine to what extent you will have to hide your real self. Hiding of self is expressed through protective/ defensive strategies.

When it is only particular expressions of your authentic self that come under attack, then it is only in those particular areas that you will hide your real self. For example, if as a male your expression of certain emotions – fear, upset, grief, sadness, loneliness – is socially blocked, then wisely you will not show these particular emotions but instead 'put on a brave face'. You may feel safe about showing other emotions such as excitement, satisfaction or anger. You may also feel safe showing the blocked emotions with certain people with whom you feel confident and loved.

When all or most attempts to express your uniqueness have been suppressed by others, then your counter-response will be to shut down totally on your authenticity. A counter-response involves recourse to protective/defensive strategies that will reduce or eliminate the threats to your being real. Whether partial or total hiding of your real self is required, you have several broad defence options: aggression/ rebel-liousness, passivity, passive-aggression, fantasy and delusion.

The rebellious or *aggressive* counter-action is an attempt to fight fire with fire, to control the suppressive behaviour of others by forcing them to back off and let you be. But because the whole focus is on how to out-manoeuvre the opposing forces, you keep taking your cues from outside yourself; as a result you remain out of contact with your own inner self.

The appeasing or *passive* response is designed to reduce the threats by conforming to outside demands, no matter how unreasonable. Your helplessness, constant appeasing of others and conformity to cultural norms are clever ploys to feed the 'monsters' that are attempting to devour either all or some of your self-expressions. The intention is to bring about a situation where 'the dog will not bite the hand that feeds it'.

As the name indicates, the *passive-aggressive* approach combines the passive and aggressive strategies. On the one hand, the person under threat acquiesces to outside control, but on the other hand, they get back at their oppressors by indirectly making life difficult for them. An example of this kind of strategy is where the woman who feels utterly dominated by her partner gives in to all his demands, but becomes physically sick or psychologically disturbed. The double protective response is truly inspired: 'See how I always try to agree with you and try to please you and look how difficult life becomes for you when you treat me badly.'

The counter-response of *fantasy* entails an avoidance of reality and an attempt to compensate in your imaginary world for all the losses experienced in reality. We all day-dream to some extent, but those individuals who live most of their lives in a dream-world have had to do so to find a way to reduce the sadness of the reality of their lives.

The counter-response of *delusion* is a sophisticated means of distorting the reality of neglect and the creation of a pseudo conviction that 'all is right with the world.' The most common delusion of all is that we have all come from happy families. A delusion that is extremely difficult to shift in psychiatry is that people's distress is purely biologically based. Individuals delude themselves that they have no problems, as do particular social systems, schools, workplaces and governments. The greater the extent of the threat, the more extensive the delusion. Delusion serves the purpose of eliminating from the conscious mind the painful experience of rejection by others of your sacred self.

There are several main ways that you can protect/defend when threats exist to your expression of your real self:

POSSIBLE COUNTER-RESPONSES

Block	Protectors				
	Aggressive	Passive	Passive-Aggressive	Fantasy	Delusion
'You're a fool.'	'Takes one to know one'; 'Fuck off.'	'Yeah, you're right'; say nothing.	You become sick; make life difficult; complain to others.	You imagine how amazingly clever you are and how the world is saved by you.	You think: 'My parents are only doing this for my own good; they're wonderful parents.'
'You're brilliant.'	'Stop putting pressure on me'; 'Back off.'	You think: 'My parents are so proud of me'; work harder.	Burnout; sickness.	You imagine being the world's best.	You think: 'I'm possessed by the devil.'
'I'm sorry you were ever born.'	'Who gives a shit what you think?'; you react violently to rejection.	You think: 'Who could ever love me?'; you stop reaching out to others.	You attempt to please but act violently towards self.	You think: 'Everybody knows about me.'	You think: 'I'm Jesus Christ.'
'You're there just for me.'	You rebel against the control.	You think: 'I live my life for you.'	You give in but get sick.	You dream of faraway places.	You think: 'I have such a happy family.'
'I'm there only for you.'	You aggressively react.	You become helpless.	You yield but become over-demanding.	You fantasise about being the hero.	You think: 'My parent(s) do everything for me.'

HIDING PARTICULAR EXPRESSIONS OF YOUR REAL SELF

Just as your unique presence may be expressed in multiple ways when safety exists, so strategies to protect your real self when threats exist take multiple forms:

- □ physical
- □ sexual
- □ emotional
- □ intellectual
- □ behavioural
- □ social
- □ creative
- □ spiritual

HIDING PHYSICAL EXPRESSION OF YOUR REAL SELF

Block to physical expression	Protectors		
	Aggressive	Passive	Passive-Aggressive
'Sit up straight.'	You throw a temper tantrum.	You conform to demand.	You conform but develop back pain.
'You're ugly.'	'You should talk, look in the mirror at yourself.'	You take on the label and take no social risks.	You accept the label but talk disparagingly to others about perpetrator.
'Eat up everything.'	You refuse to eat.	You conform to demand.	You eat up, but later on vomit.
'You're the best looking one in the family.'	'So is that supposed to make me feel good?'	You get worried, upset and go on a diet.	You take on the label but become attracted to people who would be considered 'plain'.

'Putting on weight, are we?' (said with sarcasm)	'Fuck you, you never have anything good to say.'	You cry and don't defend yourself.	You agree but stop giving your critic their favourite food.
'You drove me to hit you.'	You hit back.	You withdraw and sulk.	You think 'I must have deserved it', but become a 'weakling'.

The physical and sexual threats that individuals experience are acknowledged legally, and the laws offers some protection against such violations. However, the level of violence and sexual violations is not being reduced. This is not surprising, as laws do not reach hearts in darkness. If society is to change, strategies adopted must be holistic and non-judgmental, and must safeguard the rights of all. Strategies for change must be enlightened in the sense that they recognise that people who block the presence of others are victims themselves. Unless compassion for the perpetrator accompanies attempts to safeguard the victim, no real change will emerge.

Whilst there has been a broadening of attitudes towards different sexual orientations, in particular homosexuality, there are many forms of sexual expression that do not receive understanding and acceptance. It is an absolute requirement that no sexual expression should threaten the sacred physical and sexual boundaries of another, and it is for this reason that rape or paedophilia, for example, cannot be tolerated. But proscription of such behaviours and strong sanctioning of their occurrence must not preclude understanding and compassion.

HIDING SEXUAL EXPRESSION OF YOUR REAL SELF

Blocks to sexual expression	Protectors		
	Aggressive	Passive	Passive-Aggressive
Violation when a child.	Violence.	Repression (become asexual).	Promiscuity.
Sexual harassment.	You verbally/ physically hit back.	You put up with it.	You accept it but gossip about perpetrator.
Sexual 'put down' from work colleague.	'Put down' in return.	You become embarrassed and withdraw.	You say nothing but go absent from work.
Treated as sexual object by partner.	Taunt partner about inadequacies.	You lie back and take it.	You accept it but take and give no pleasure during sexual encounter.
Uninvited sexual exposure by another.	Laugh and ridicule.	You walk away.	You do nothing, but become inefficient at work.
Rape	Murder	Block out the memory of the rape.	Repress and have total loss of libido.

Your protectors are always right; they are a measure of your distance from self as a result of a lack of safety; the latter may be the result of little or no back-up systems in the surrounding culture to deal with neglect. Even when you are in possession of your sacred self, recourse to protective action may sometimes be required, for example in the case of rape. The difference in protection between the person who is real and the person who is hidden is that in the first case the protective action comes from a strong sense of personal worthiness and includes a straightforward demand from society for safety from violations, whereas the protectors of the person in shadow do not spring from such a place of clarity and directness.

Whilst society now accepts that both children and adults can be physically and sexually hurt, people have not matured sufficiently to acknowledge that children and adults are also emotionally hurt frequently, intensely and enduringly. Indeed it is often the case that physical and sexual hurts take place in a sea of emotional neglect.

HIDING EMOTIONAL EXPRESSION OF YOUR REAL SELF

There is the notion that it is difficult to measure emotional hurt and in turn to legislate for it. This is not true; the measures for emotional hurt include fear, depression, stress, psycho-somatic illnesses, avoidance, timidity, aggression, physical pain, insomnia and absenteeism from work.

Block to emotional expression	Protectors		
	Aggressive	Passive	Passive-Aggressive
'Stop crying.'	You scream: 'You never listen!'	You choke down tears.	You suppress upset and become depressed.
'Pull yourself together.'	'You're a great fucking help.'	You bottle up feelings.	You stop communicating and take to heavy drinking.
'Don't be angry.'	'Why – can't you cope?'	You swallow anger.	You bury your anger and take to confiding in another.
'Don't go all sloppy (loving) on me.'	'You hate me, don't you?'	You stop showing warmth.	You hold back affection and start extra-marital relationship.
'Not afraid again, are we?' (said in sarcastic tone of voice)	'What are you, my bloody analyst?'	You hide fears.	You suppress fears and withdraw affection.

HIDING INTELLECTUAL EXPRESSION OF YOUR REAL SELF

There is little recognition of the hurt that children and adults suffer around the intellectual expression of self. Most people experience considerable ridicule of their intellectual expression, due in many cases to confusion of knowledge with intelligence and the use of knowledge as a means of feeling superior and making others feel inferior. There are multiple types of knowledge, only some of which are valued and prized, but there is only one vast reservoir of intellectual potential in each person.

Block to emotional expression	Protectors		
	Aggressive	Passive	Passive-Aggressive
'You're a fool.'	'It takes one to know one.'	You take on the label: 'Yes, you're right. I am a fool.'	You accept judgment and make no further effort to learn.
'Don't be too smart.'	'Why, because you might be shown up?'	You hide your intelligence by non-expression of your opinions.	You say nothing and begin to show low attainment.
'You're brilliant.'	'Stop putting pressure on me.'	You take on label by putting major pressure on yourself to live up to it.	You accept label and develop anorexia nervosa.
'There is only one way to do this.'	'You mean it has to be your way.'	You conform.	You conform and become helpless.
'What would you know about anything?'	'It wouldn't be hard to know more than you.'	You go silent.	You swallow hurt and become depressed.
'A monkey would know the answer.'	'You're so fucking smart yourself!'	You keep trying to find answer.	You say nothing and reduce contact with this person.

HIDING BEHAVIOURAL EXPRESSION OF YOUR REAL SELF

Behaviour is the wonderful means we have of testing reality and acquiring knowledge and skills to live in the complex worlds we encounter. Life is an adventure, but for so many people it becomes a test, a fearful task, a chore, something to be got through. Criticism, sarcasm, cynicism, aggression, punishment, humiliation − these are but some of the reactions individuals experience to their attempts to explore their worlds. The fear of failure, the fear of success and the addiction to success are all products of the need to protect against ridicule and pressure around behavioural perform-ance. Sadly, so many adults, parents and teachers put the emphasis on the result rather than the wonderful process of learning. Performance anxiety is rampant in homes, schools, workplaces and sports fields. In response, many people settle for the average, thereby lowering other people's expectations of them and eliminating the possibilities of failure. Although a high percentage of both second and third-level students drop out of courses, the educational system still does not accept that as long as learning is a source of emotional, social and intellectual threat, no progress will be made in restoring the eagerness to learn that is present in all infants. During my years in a monastery, I recall taking up tennis and playing an accomplished player and losing 6-0. One of the priests watching made the public comment, 'Did you not even win one game?' I remember feeling humiliated and extremely angry; it wasn't until many years later that I took up tennis again.

The valuing of individuals not for their unique and sacred person but for what they do is a darkening process and leads to protective reactions such as depression, parasuicide (an attempt to bring other people's attention to inner distress), suicide, high anxiety, inferiority or superiority, perfectionism, addiction to success, extreme apathy and violence. When the sacredness of the enduring presence of a human being becomes less important than a bit of transient behaviour, it is equivalent to soul murder.

Block to behavioural expression	Protectors		
	Aggressive	Passive	Passive-Aggressive
'Wrong, wrong, wrong!'	'Well then, do it yourself, you moron.'	You try harder.	You keep trying and complain to others.
'You call that an effort?'	'Who asked your opinion?'	You increase effort.	You keep effort up and become timid and fearful.
'If you can't do it right, don't do it at all.'	'Fine, then do it yourself.'	You try to prove yourself.	You become a perfectionist and socially isolated.
'Do you ever win?'	'What's it to you?'	'I'll show them.'	You keep trying and avoid critic's company.
'Is this the best you can do?'	'So, you can do better?'	You push yourself harder.	You conform but get frequently sick.
'What a failure you are.'	'You're no bloody genius yourself.'	You become a perfectionist.	You push yourself harder and show the other person up when the opportunity arises.

HIDING SOCIAL EXPRESSION OF YOUR REAL SELF

The social presence of each person is a unique and sacred phenomenon that deserves recognition. It is equally important that when a person is absent from a social system (family, work, club, community), their absence is recognised when they return. Many housewives, parents, teachers, students and workers complain about feeling anonymous, not being seen, not being appreciated and not being celebrated. Our difference from others is what marks the presence of each person, but the pressure to conform demeans and lessens the presence of many people. Strong protectors are required to reduce the hurt caused by the darkening of an individual's presence and the different expressions of self.

Block to social expression	Protectors		
	Aggressive	Passive	Passive-Aggressive
Ignoring your presence.	You verbally or physically attack the person.	You walk away.	You withdraw and break off contact.
Bullying you.	You bully in return.	You say nothing to anyone.	You do nothing and secretly get back at the bully.
Putting you down in public.	You create a scene.	You bottle up anger.	You keep your head down and never return to that particular scene again.
Hostile nicknaming.	You counter nickname.	You take on role (for example, play the 'fool', be the 'clown', act 'stupid').	You say nothing but look out for ways of putting them down behind their backs.
Not including you.	You say sarcastically 'Am I the invisible man here?'	You slink away.	You feel deflated and afterwards gossip about the person's rudeness.
You witness another person being humiliated.	You react: 'Who in the hell do you think you are treating a person in this way?'	You turn a blind eye.	You do nothing and later collude with gossip about the person.

It is not only direct blocks that result in your hiding the targeted aspect of yourself, but indirect blocks can also lead to a similar response. It is well known that when children witness others children being physically, sexually, emotionally, intellectually or socially violated, they learn quickly to mask that aspect of self that is not safe to show. In the workplace, employees tend to take their cue from leaders, and when leaders are neglectful of self and others, employees quickly learn to close down on those areas of self that are a source of threat to these leaders. Children also watch how adults react and assess very quickly what aspects of themselves they need to hide.

HIDING CREATIVE EXPRESSION OF YOUR REAL SELF

Creativity is the mark of a revelation of each person's uniqueness. Whether you operate from the real or the shadow self, you always do it in a way that is different. Because of the pressures to conform, the survival response is to try to be the same as others, but there is always a creativity in the way each family member conforms. For example, in a family with four children where there are pressures to conform, one child becomes the high academic achiever, the other the charmer and joker, the other the rebel and the fourth the one who takes care of everyone in the family. Each child in this family has found a creative way to reduce blows to their presence by behaving in ways that are conformist but nonetheless different. It is important to realise that the child who rebels is also conformist because he continues to take his cues for his reactions from others, especially his parents. However, when creativity is employed as a protective force, it is severely limited because it serves a survival rather than a dynamic and progressive purpose.

Block to creative expression	Protectors		
	Aggressive	Passive	Passive-Aggressive
'This is not the way to paint the sun.'	'You're just a narrow-minded teacher.'	'Well, show me the right way.'	You say nothing but drop out of art class.
'Where did you hear that rubbish that you are here to live your own life?'	'You're full of shit.'	You go silent.	You conform but get sick.
'I wouldn't show that verse to anybody else.'	'I'm just sorry I showed it to you, you insensitive pig.'	'You're right.'	You stop writing and break off contact.
'Trying to be different, are we?'	'With a stick-in-the-mud like you, that would not be difficult.'	You hide your creativity.	You conform and look out for another job.
'Just do what you've been shown.'	'What are you afraid of – intelligence?'	You yield.	You conform and act stupid.
'Why aren't you like other people?'	'That's your problem, not mine.'	You give them what they want.	You conform and denigrate their profession.

I remember in my early professional life as a clinical psychologist hearing the comment 'Why aren't you like other psychologists?' because I refused to do so-called 'personality' and other psychometric tests. My response to the psychiatrists making the comment was that if they did not like my manner of assessment – which was to listen to the client's story – then they should not send clients to me. I was determined to treat clients as individuals, worthy of being loved, listened to and understood.

HIDING SPIRITUAL EXPRESSION OF YOUR REAL SELF

The need to hide the spiritual expression of self can arise from many sources — religious and spiritual oppression, ridicule, lack of support and lack of safe opportunities to reveal your deeper nature. I have been privileged to work with people who had amazing 'out of body' experiences which had removed all fear of death and given them a deep sense of their deathless and powerful spirit, but which they had dared not previously reveal for fear of ridicule and being labelled as crazy.

Block to spiritual expression	Protectors		
	Aggressive	Passive	Passive-Aggressive
'Catholicism is a joke.'	You verbally fight to convince your opponent.	You determine never to talk about it again.	You go silent and gossip about the person to others.
'Women don't count in the Church's eyes.'	You aggressively fight for equality for women in the Church.	You conform.	You say nothing and reduce church attendance.
'Belief in religion will not be tolerated here.'	You join radical, militarist 'spiritual' group.	You go underground.	You yield and join underground radical movement.
'You should accept what the Church teaches.'	You rebel.	You conform.	You say nothing and just don't attend church.
'You attend church with us and that's that.'	You join an 'alternative' sect.	You follow the prescript.	You conform and when out of sight do your own thing.

In most Western countries, the demands by family, school, community and state to practise the 'state religion' have weakened considerably. Indeed, the new pressure to be materialistic has made money-making and being a success the new religious practices. 'Having' has become the insidious enemy of spirituality.

WHEN YOU HIDE, OTHERS HIDE TOO

For many years of my life I had always sought to be there and care for others, but in the process I kept others around me helpless and dependent. When you operate from a place of protection, as in my over-caring behaviour, others around you who are also in shadow will respond with their own protective behaviours such as, in my case, helplessness and dependence. The other person knows (consciously or unconsciously) that if she were to expose or object to or refuse to co-operate with your protective behaviour, she would be rejected. The difficulty of saying 'no' to a parent or friend or partner who lives her life through you, is something most of us have experienced. But when you do not say 'no', the real need to be responsible for yourself is shadowed in favour of allowing the other person to take care of you. Both parties in the relationship are now dependent and are hiding important aspects of themselves — the need to receive and the need to give.

In the case of the protective behaviour of aggression, the typical protective response of the other person is to give in, allow you have your own way 'for peace sake' and forego her own needs, beliefs and opinions. Both parties are now operating from a hidden place. If the other person were strongly in her own presence, her response would be authentic and respectful of herself and of you, rather than capitulation. The risks of being real in an aggressive situation are high — an escalation of the aggression, the possibility of violence, further rejection, possibilities of the aggressor hurting themselves in order to force conformity. However, the risks of not being real are even greater — loss of authenticity, co-dependence in the relationship, denial of difference, creativity and sacredness, and entrapment in a shadow world.

Begin to notice how you respond to the shadow behaviours of others: whether in turn you hide an aspect of yourself or whether you express what is really happening in you.

Shadow behaviour	Protective response	Real response
'Let me do that for you.'	'Sure, why not.'	'Thank you, but I prefer to do it myself.'
'You're wrong.'	'Yes, you're right.'	'We appear to have a difference in opinion here.'
'Mend my life.'	'What is it that you need?'	'I am not responsible for your life.'
'I'm taking the car.'	'Of course, go ahead.'	'I need to check whether or not that suits.'
'You're always late.'	'Sorry, sorry.'	'I apologise for being late now, but I am not always late.'
'I'm painting the bedroom white.'	'Oh great.'	'White would not be my choice, I would like to discuss other colours.'
Your partner screams at you.	You scream back.	You show no response.

To confront someone who is in darkness with the light of your realness is an act of love of self and the other person; it provides the opportunity for both individuals to experience being real.

You need to be close to your true self to be able to withstand the protective responses of the other person. The challenge for us is to come into the light; a challenge that when taken up not only enriches ourselves but allows others around us to emerge from the shadows also.

CHAPTER FIVE
THE SHADOW SELF

THE REAL SELF AND THE SHADOW SELF

The shadow self is the sum of all the particular protectors you have developed to hide some or all aspects of your real self; these hidden aspects will only emerge when emotional and social safety is present. It is with the shadow self we most identify, through labels such as 'I am a man, an Irishman, a Corkman, a husband, a friend, a psychologist, a writer, I am a radical, a negotiator, kind, tough, ruthless, a businessman, caring, resolute, non-conformist, "a winner", spiritual and so on.' What is enthralling about the shadow definitions is that you will not go contrary to your descriptions of self and this brings you into a world of limitations. Hidden behind your uni-polarised ways of being in the world are subconscious fears of acting in the opposite ways. I know from my own experience that when I found myself being insensitive and uncaring it shook me to my core, and when such 'aberrations' occurred I would do all in my power to reinstate my 'carer' image. Similarly, for the person who has a tough image, any display of 'softness' will threaten his protective ploy, and he will quickly restore his 'hard man' identity. The real self has nothing to do with labels. The real self unconsciously knows its uniqueness, sacredness and limitless potential and, when it is safe to do so, will act out spontaneously and authentically from that powerful place.

Your authentic self is the realisation of your unique and sacred being. Your real self is there from the beginning, but because experiences in your world lead your real self to be eclipsed, much of your life-journey is the road back to self. The shadow self is an illusion, a necessary protection, but unless *under*stood, can lead to an extremely limited existence or illness or premature death. Individuals whose shadow self is identified primarily with their work are at high risk of sickness or death when they retire. Similarly the person who identifies herself with her partner in life is at risk of dying herself if her spouse passes away.

There are two important aspects to understand about the world of the shadow self. The first is that there are two levels to the shadow — the conscious and the subconscious. Second, and connected to this conscious/subconscious nature, is that the shadow self is both a shield that protects the real self and a mirror that reflects the challenges involved in reconnecting with your real self. There is no weakness or lack of intelligence in the formation of the shadow self, and there is no wisdom in attempting to change it; rather the wisdom lies in understanding and working with the shadow self.

CONSCIOUS AND SUBCONSCIOUS DIMENSIONS OF THE SHADOW SELF

When threats exist to the expression of your real self, unless you are in a place of solid possession of your self, you will react protectively to reduce the threat. You may guard yourself automatically, but it is a conscious act. The threat itself exists at the subconscious level. For example, if in a group of friends, one person dismisses an opinion of yours and you react defensively with verbal aggression: 'What the fuck makes you an expert?', you know you are being aggressive as the response leaves your mouth. Later on, when somebody says 'you went a bit over the top with Tom', you will tend to admit it, but add defensively 'he needed somebody to take him down a peg'. Your defensive responses show that you are not ready to consciously see the subconscious threat and free yourself of the addiction to what other people think or say about you.

Underneath the conscious act is the subconscious issue; in this example the issue is that you hate any form of criticism. Your challenge is not to force yourself to stop being aggressive but to learn how not to be threatened by criticism. Taking the threat out of criticism — by recognising it as a message from the other person about themselves — is what will extinguish the shadow behaviour of aggression. The aggressive behaviour acted as a protective shield for you, and it also mirrored for you the vulnerability that needed to be healed.

The conscious dimension of the shadow self serves you very well — it keeps a solid shield around what you dare not express about your real and sacred presence. The behaviours that you consciously employ to protect yourself — even though they may be troublesome, as in the example above — are less threatening than facing the vulnerabilities that are there in the subconscious shadow world. Suppose you have a 'macho' shadow self that is hiding a subconscious fear of demonstrating a need to be nurtured. You probably will have difficulty in admitting to your 'hard man' image, but if some astute person should see through to what you dare not express, you may very well respond with aggression, cynicism, sarcasm or avoidance of that person. Such reactions reflect the fact that you are not ready to explore your underworld of vulnerability.

However, there is a deeper part of your self that pushes for the subconscious shadow self to be revealed and the vulnerabilities therein to be healed so that progress towards unity with your real self is attained. This deeper part lies in the unconscious, which is the heart of spirituality and physical, psychological and social harmony. This unconscious power finds amazing ways to make visible the subconscious vulnerabilities of the shadow self so that, when the time is right, you can touch into the resources for healing that have always been there in you. What is most hidden in you is what you attract into your life! For example, in my own life my conscious shadow self was to be 'the carer'; this was my protective shield against my subconscious vulnerability around asking for care for myself. The people I most attracted into my life were those in need of care who reflected my own hidden need. Even the professions I took up – priesthood, teaching and clinical psychology – were projections from my unconscious to try to make visible my terror of asking anything for myself and the resultant distancing from my real self. We cannot be free to be our real selves unless we can go to both poles of the continuum of any behaviour – in this case care for others and care for self.

In my fear of showing my real self – I needed to receive care as well as give care – I found a shadowy way of trying to get the message across: 'Surely if I show so much care, you will see my need for care.' When I am in possession of myself I can ask directly for that care.

A pattern I frequently observe when the level of threat is great is that the protective actions at the conscious level are the exact opposite of the vulnerabilities at the subconscious level, as in the example of the 'macho' man who is vulnerable around his need for nurturance. The pattern also applies to the example from my own life whereby the protective actions at the conscious level of the compulsion 'to give' to others were opposite to the vulnerabilities at the subconscious level, which were fear of receiving.

Conscious shadow behaviour	Possible sub-conscious shadow fears (what lies hidden)
☐ being aggressive	☐ fear of showing vulnerability
☐ always caring for others	☐ fearful of asking care for self
☐ constantly complaining	☐ fearful of expressing importance
☐ being fearful	☐ fear of demonstrating anger
☐ being the 'funny man'	☐ fearful around the need to be serious
☐ being manipulative	☐ fearful of asking directly for what you need
☐ being mean	☐ fearful of not being good enough
☐ being passive	☐ vulnerable about feeling 'I count'
☐ being perfectionist	☐ frightened of failure
☐ being rigid	☐ fearful of being wrong
☐ being shy	☐ afraid to show power

It can be seen that the challenge lies not in changing your conscious shadow behaviours but in expressing what lies hidden in the subconscious shadow world. When the latter happens, equilibrium emerges and the conscious shadow behaviours broaden to a free, open and non-threatening level of expression of your real self.

WHAT IS HIDDEN IS CONSTANTLY BEING REVEALED

It is as a result of our wisdom that our hidden vulnerabilities are constantly either being mirrored back to us or being projected onto other people, objects or the world. This process exists so that we may become aware of what lies hidden.

Mirroring is the phenomenon whereby people tend to attract someone opposite to their shadow definition of self. For example, people who describe themselves as passive very often attract partners and friends and bosses who are aggressive and dominant. Wonderfully, this wise unconscious part of the mind finds a way to present the necessary challenge of accepting and expressing one's own hidden anger and power, but not in the defensive way used by those who are aggressive.

The things we do not want to be, do not want to see inside ourselves, do not want to live out, do not want to describe ourselves as, we encounter frequently in the significant relationships in our lives. Where both people in the relationship are in shadow, the consequence is conflict, in that each person attempts to control the other by judging, sulking, withdrawing, manipulating, engaging in hostile silences, forcing and blaming behaviours. Ironically, it is only by accepting in yourself the very behaviours that you condemn in the other person that any possibility of harmony is attainable. The person opposite to you in their 'I' definitions offers you a glorious opportunity for resolving this hidden part of yourself. It is not that you go to the extreme pole of the behaviour you reject in the other; the idea is to find the golden mean between the extremes of behaviour shown by the two of you. For example, if you find yourself being very critical of a partner, friend or colleague

whom you regard as 'lazy' and 'irresponsible', the challenge for you is not to be lazy yourself, but it may be that you need to allow yourself to rest and let go of having to always be the responsible one. The challenge for the partner, friend or colleague who is opposite to you in their protective behaviour, is to risk taking on responsibility and showing initiative. Once you begin to do what you dare not do, the see-saw of extreme behaviours of laziness and compulsive responsibility-taking becomes balanced by responsibility on the one side and freedom to rest, relax and to be at ease on the other side.

Projection is another unconscious means by which your rejection of certain aspects of your real self is revealed to you. Projection is a process whereby that which lies hidden is uncannily projected onto something outside ourselves — God, evil, parents, partners, boss, friends, atheists, hedonists, aliens. How often do we hear ourselves say:

- □ 'There can be no God when people can do such violent things.'
- □ 'Money is the source of all evil.'
- □ 'No wonder I lose control at times, look at how my parents were.'
- □ 'You would drive a saint to drink.'
- □ 'People are just out to exploit you.'
- □ 'When you most need friends, they let you down.'
- □ 'The world is "gone to pot" because nobody believes in anything anymore.'
- □ 'People are just out for themselves.'
- □ 'Forces outside myself drove me to perpetrate that sexual abuse.'

When you look closely at each of these projections you begin to see what it is that we dare not admit to within ourselves:

- ☐ 'I dare not feel violent.'
- ☐ 'I could not admit to having any "evil" impulses.'
- ☐ 'Losing control threatens me.'
- ☐ 'Taking responsibility for my own wrongdoing frightens me.'
- ☐ 'I would be terrified to say I could not be there for someone.'
- ☐ 'I am afraid to depend on myself.'
- ☐ 'Not to believe in something would terrify me.'
- ☐ 'I couldn't possibly ask for anything for myself.'
- ☐ 'Having "abnormal" sexual attractions scare me.'

It is only by getting to grips with the vulnerabilities we deny in ourselves that we can get what we hope for — unity with self and others.

Illness can be another means of projecting outward the hidden dis-ease inside self. For example, back pain can symbolically represent the hidden issues of 'backing out of confrontation' or 'taking too much on your back'. Anorexia nervosa may symbolise being starved of love or lack of freedom to be oneself. Heart disease may carry messages related to being 'heartless', or 'heart scalded', or the crying need for a heart response to you from significant others. Cancer may represent what is eating you up inside yourself that you dare not express. Migraine headache may symbolise rigidity and being constantly uptight because of always having to be the best at everything you do.

Many people find it threatening to reveal freely and honestly their deepest problems, yet they will recount willingly their bodily symptoms, not seeing that these symptoms are revealing aspects of what it is that they wanted so much to remain hidden. But we will only avail of the opportunities for being authentic that illness presents us when it is emotionally and socially safe for us to talk about the deeper dis-ease. There is no doubt that illness has the effect of softening people up, thereby reducing possibilities of rejection. Illness invites us to be real and in turn invites others to be real in their responses. How many times have we had the experience where serious illness shattered the illusions of public image, success addictions, or co-dependencies and led to people being real with each other. In times of crisis, such as war, famine or natural disaster, people can often be there for each other in a very real way, whereas peacetime does not automatically mean *real* time between people.

THE LIGHT CREATES THE SHADOW

The typical answer to the question 'Who or what creates the shadow self?' is: 'People who are unloving and neglectful', or 'adverse circumstances' (for example, poverty, unemployment, political or religious oppression). This is a clever projection, which allows responsibility to be taken away from the self. But it is the light that creates the shadow or, in other words, it is your real self that develops your screen self. When you understand this, you are in a position to use the vast powers you use to hide your self away to instead make your real presence felt.

Human beings are not passive recipients of what happens to them, be it of an affirming or a threatening nature. You adjust your shadow behaviours to match different people and different situations. You know intuitively when you can remain true to your real self and when you need to close down on a particular aspect of your authentic self. A young woman once told me that her father had reared her to 'kill off all feelings', and she cleverly learned not to express or show those taboo emotions in his presence. However, when she felt it was safe, she did show her emotional side to others. When I first met her she was inclined to stay stuck in blame of her father for her emotional reticence, but she became empowered when she saw it was she who had chosen this way of coping with her father's fear of emotion. Only with this understanding of herself could she take on the challenge of being emotionally real with her father and other people in a similar shadow place. She was also able to free herself when she realised that it was not her father but herself she needed to convince about the maturity of being emotionally authentic. Had she attempted to persuade her father of the importance of emotions, she would still be projecting responsibility on to him and would still be looking for permission from him to be free in her shut-down area of self-expression. Furthermore, she would have been attempting to counter-control, to get him to see things her way, and nothing would more surely have increased her father's defensive strategies. Communication is about getting through to yourself; you need to convince yourself of the wisdom of being authentic.

You might rightly ask: How is it that there are so many people who, in spite of attempts to lovingly care for them, remain imprisoned in their shadow selves? When you have suffered great loss of loving, gross neglect and maybe physical and sexual violence, the defences you build around your sacred self are powerful, and wisely it is going to take a lot of patience and endurance on the part of others if you are going to risk showing even a glimpse of your real self. Regrettably, very often people are not in such a place of light to offer such patient love and compassion to others. A phrase that keeps me going at times of despairing that a client will ever open up to receiving love is 'I will wait patiently for an eternity for you to become present to yourself'. When I lose patience (my shadow response), I lose ground with my clients, and rightly so; they withdraw even deeper into shadows of self-dejection. The fact that it is the light of your real self that creates the shadow self is grounds for power, hope and optimism. It means you have always been taking care of yourself in the most amazing, though dark, ways and that process will change direction towards the light when you find sufficient support inside and outside yourself. The road less travelled – to being real – is avoided not because people do not want to come home to themselves, but because it is dangerous to make the U (you) turn back to self. Not too many people are on the corner, cheering and supporting us when we begin the journey inwards, whereas there are many who put pressure on us to remain on the shadowed road most travelled.

WHEN SHADOW BEHAVIOURS HURT OTHERS

In my practice I have come across the tragedy where a parent has not only taken their own life but also the lives of children. On a lesser, though still tragic level I have encountered adults who have physically mutilated partners, neighbours or friends, and parents who have physically and sexually violated their children. Where is the love in all of this? I have agonised over this issue for a long time. It is clear from my own life that when I felt inferior I lashed out violently to reduce the other person whose behaviour was a source of threat. The purpose of the aggressive outbursts was to protect myself, not to hurt others.

The intention of shadow behaviours is to hide some or all aspects of your real self from whatever threatens your presence; and so it is an attempted act of care of yourself. There may also be an intention to protect others from perceived threat, as in the case of the mother who poisons her children before poisoning herself — her subconscious intention for herself is to remove herself from all threats to expression of her real self; her intention for her children is to remove them from a world that she believes will hurt and neglect them as it has done to her. The intention to protect others is also evident in the situation where parents overprotect children — their subconscious intention for themselves is to be needed so they will be loved, and their intention for their children is to ensure they do not experience the perceived hurt that can result in taking on challenges. I remember a very well-groomed young woman approaching me and asking me, 'Is it true if you have been sexually abused, then as an adult you will repeat the neglect?' I told her that this may or may not happen but, I said, what is more likely to happen is the reaction of determination to control things so that your children will not suffer the same fate. It emerged that she never let her two children out of her sight, would never leave them alone with an adult, not even grandparents. While her intention was to protect, unfortunately her over-protection was causing major levels of social and emotional helplessness in her children. The young woman subsequently went on to explore ways in which she could empower her children to safeguard their own physical and sexual integrity and for herself to evaluate risk more realistically.

It is easier to see that the intention of shadow behaviours is to protect and not hurt in the examples given above than it is in situations where people torture others, or squander all the family income so that children and spouse go hungry, or where the majority in a country engage in 'ethnic cleansing' of a minority. But the greater the shadow behaviour, the greater the hidden insecurities. In cases such as 'ethnic cleansing', where one group of people are in fear of their lives and have experienced obliteration of their culture and exploitation, sometimes for centuries, the shadow behaviour of getting rid of the perceived terrible enemy allows not even a pinprick of light to penetrate the darkness. Any feelings of empathy or regard for the 'enemy' would mean not only a weakening of the shadow weapon but would also increase the risk of annihilation. Unless structures are created wherein both threatened parties can begin to value self and each other, accept differences, tolerate each other's cultures and practise equality, then the darkness of hate and murder will continue.

CHAPTER SIX
SHADOW PROFILES

Each person's shadow selves are creations that reflect their uniqueness and their unrepeatable biographical experiences. People often ask, 'How is it that children born and reared in the same family and all treated the same emerge so differently?' The truth is that no two children are reared in the same family; family dynamics are constantly changing, as are the parents themselves and the relationship between them. Furthermore, subconsciously each parent responds uniquely to each child, and the gender of a child can have a profound influence on the nature of parental involvement. But the most significant factor is that each child within the family has a fierce determination to express his or her own individuality, and ingeniously finds unique ways to express difference. Because no parents are without shadow, children are under threat and must develop a false persona to protect against anything that lessens their presence. Generally speaking, these early protective mechanisms persist into adulthood. Should circumstances change for better or worse, either within the person or in the cultures experienced, the shadow self will be adjusted accordingly. The experience in adulthood of cultures different to those in which you were reared can present opportunities for breaking free of shackles that prevent you being yourself, or you may encounter someone who persists in his or her regard and devotion to you, thereby creating safety for you to be more authentic. Of course it is also true that adult experiences of cultures and people can be of a nature that reinforces old defences and may require new protectors against new threats to being yourself. For example, you may feel anonymous in your workplace or you may have married a person who constantly puts you down.

Within the infinite array of shadow selves, it is possible to identify some common themes and to describe some profiles. Bear in mind that nobody fits one of these profiles in its entirety, but aspects of the profile may fit you at different times and in different circumstances. When examining the different profiles outlined below, keep in mind the aspects of your shadow self that are peculiar to you and also remember that 'in a world of individuals it makes no sense to compare'. Furthermore, even though some people may use the same label or labels to describe themselves, the reasons why they have come to that shadowed place are likely to be unique and the hidden challenges totally different. It is important too to appreciate that there are times when you do operate out of a free and authentic place and that your unconscious keeps presenting you with opportunities to be real, no matter where you are or whom you are with.

In parentheses alongside each label listed below is the possible hidden issue that lies at the heart of your darkened state. The various labels are grouped under different headings: physical, behavioural, emotional, social, intellectual and creative.

The benefits of examining these labels and profiles are:

- the development of a conscious awareness of how you typically describe yourself
- the opportunity to detect what aspects of your real self are hidden
- the creation of a platform for authenticity

A good lead into assessing the nature of your shadow self is to ask yourself and a trustworthy other: 'What word(s) would you use to describe me?' The list below presents the most common possibilities, but answer the question before you consult the list. The shadow definitions given are not exhaustive. It may be educational to hold back your definition(s) until your partner reveals his or her word(s). Do not be too quick to dismiss your own description in the face of a different one from your partner. All sorts of possibilities may account for the difference — projection by your partner of some hidden needs he or she has of you, or denial on your part that you could act in such a way, or a delusion on your part that you accurately fit your own one-word description of yourself. What is important is that both definitions carry reliable information about where you (and your partner) are right now, and what is required is acceptance and not conflict. Acceptance is the cornerstone of challenging any definition that limits your expressiveness as a person.

PHYSICAL SHADOW LABELS

Label

- ☐ 'Sickly' ('If I'm well I'm terrified of not being seen')
- ☐ 'Athletic' ('I am terrified of showing intellectual aspects of myself')
- ☐ 'Handsome/beautiful' (I'm afraid if I'm not good-looking I won't be loved')
- ☐ 'Hypochondriacal' ('There is a lot of emotional pain I am afraid to talk about')
- ☐ 'Anorexic' ('I'm starved of love')

The body never lies and, when truly listened to, provides an amazing window into the hidden world of children and adults. Children, in particular, are masters at employing their bodies to protect themselves from further hurt. However, when a constellation of 'sickly' protectors form and the child begins to be seen by parents and others as 'the weak one' or 'the fragile one', then serious questions about the family dynamics need to be addressed. For example, does sickness reduce harshness, or does sickness produce more care, or does being ill reduce conflict?

BEHAVIOURAL SHADOW LABELS

Label

- ☐ 'Perfectionist' ('I'm in terror of failure')
- ☐ 'Devil-may-care' ('I'm in terror of responsibility')
- ☐ 'Wanderer' ('I'm frightened of commitment')
- ☐ 'Carer' ('I dare not ask for anything for myself')
- ☐ 'Rescuer' ('I'm frightened to say that I need help')
- ☐ 'Drop-out' ('I'm terrified of not being loved')
- ☐ 'Passive' ('I must not assert my presence')
- ☐ 'Aggressive' ('I'm petrified of not being seen')
- ☐ 'Competitive' ('I can't take failure')
- ☐ 'Dictator' ('I have no real sense of myself')
- ☐ 'Workaholic' ('I'm scared to be')
- ☐ 'Spendthrift' ('I'm afraid to assert my unique value')
- ☐ 'Hedonist' ('I don't matter')
- ☐ 'Controller' ('I'm frightened of being spontaneous and open')

Behavioural labels are the most commonly used, as it is only recently that more openness is developing around emotional expression and emotional receptivity. However, it is females who have become more emotionally literate; men still struggle with being in touch with their feelings.

EMOTIONAL SHADOW LABELS

Label

- ☐ 'Neurotic' ('It is not one bit safe to be myself')
- ☐ 'Timid' ('I dare not show how powerful I am')
- ☐ 'Shy' ('I'm not at all certain of being liked)
- ☐ 'Lost little girl/boy' ('It's not safe to be in charge of my own life')
- ☐ 'Extrovert' ('My inner world frightens me')
- ☐ 'Introvert' ('The outer world frightens me')
- ☐ 'Sensitive' ('I'm afraid of letting my guard down')
- ☐ 'Cold fish' ('It's too daunting to give any sign that I feel things')
- ☐ 'Earth mother' ('I must not be there for myself')
- ☐ 'Wimp' ('My deepest fear is to show that I am powerful')
- ☐ 'Histrionic' ('I'm terrified of being left alone')
- ☐ 'Martyr' ('I must not enjoy myself')

Nowadays there is a trend that 'being in your feelings' is essential to personal growth and that those who live in their heads or are always 'busy' are further back on the road than those who are more in touch with their feelings. Whilst feelings are a powerful way into the realisation of self, dreams, actions, thoughts, art, poetry, sickness are equally powerful ways to access the core of your being.

SOCIAL SHADOW LABELS

Label

- ☐ 'Superior' ('I'm afraid of not being good enough')
- ☐ 'Inferior' ('It's too frightening to demand equality')
- ☐ 'Actor' ('I dare not show my true self')
- ☐ 'Rebel' ('I don't want to show how insecure I am')

- ☐ 'Feminist' ('It's not safe to show my vulnerable side')
- ☐ 'Macho' ('It's not safe to show my feminine side')
- ☐ 'Socialite' ('I can't be alone')
- ☐ 'Loner' ('People threaten me')
- ☐ 'Charmer' ('Nobody could love me for myself')
- ☐ 'Homebird' ('I'm terrified of being free')
- ☐ 'Comedian' ('There's much about myself I do not show')
- ☐ 'Snob' ('I'm afraid people will look down their noses at me')

It is not surprising how familiar these social shadow labels sound, because whether we are in or out of relationships, so much of what we do is a reaction to those around us. Indeed, relationships are frequently the mirror of how we define ourselves.

SEXUAL SHADOW LABELS

Label

- ☐ 'Don Juan'/Femme fatale ('I'm afraid of being on my own')
- ☐ 'Gigolo' ('Without sexual prowess I am nothing')
- ☐ 'Sexpot' ('I'm so much afraid to say how much I need to be held')
- ☐ 'Frigid' ('I am emotionally frozen')
- ☐ 'Impotent' ('Power frightens me')

Many unresolved vulnerabilities are expressed through sexuality. Sexuality is a powerful drive, and because it is not life-threatening when used as a defence (like withholding food or water) it is a less threatening weapon to use in the hide-and-seek war of the expression of self.

INTELLECTUAL SHADOW LABELS

Label

- ☐ 'Radical' ('I'm afraid to be the same')
- ☐ 'Conservative' ('It is too frightening to be different')
- ☐ 'Critic' ('I hate myself')
- ☐ 'Bookworm' (Feelings threaten me')
- ☐ 'Genius' ('Failure frightens me')
- ☐ 'Swot' ('I'm afraid to feel')

Many men attempt to be seen through 'being intellectual'. I recall projecting an 'intellectual persona' in my mid-twenties, with dark clothes, beard, pipe, book in hand, only to be found in dark corners. What I was terrified of was that nobody would find me physically and sexually attractive. The latter were the key hidden challenges I needed to face.

CREATIVE SHADOW LABELS

Label

- ☐ 'Artistic' ('There is more to me than my creations, but I'm afraid to express those aspects of me')
- ☐ 'Way-out' ('I'm afraid to be in touch with the pain of not being loved')
- ☐ 'Inventive' (I'm afraid that if I do not keep inventing new things I will not be of any value')

Labels coming under the 'creative' classification tend to be fewer due to the fact that most relationships and cultures demand conformity and punish difference.

It is vital to appreciate the power of either self-labelling or labelling by others. The powerful purpose behind labelling self is to get people to see and respond to you in a certain way. For example, when you define yourself as a 'carer', what you want is people to make demands on you, to need you, so that you can establish a defensive zone around your terror of asking anything for yourself. Similarly, the 'bully' wants to make people afraid of him, so that demands that would threaten his hidden world of not being good enough are not made of him. Sometimes when another person puts a label on you, for instance 'radical', they are now determining their reaction to you — basically not to listen — because what you are saying is touching into their hidden world of being afraid to be different.

People who are mature do not label, are not unduly threatened, are willing to listen to alternative views and, in the end, will make up their own minds on the issues being discussed. Because they have their own solid base of accept-ance of self, they have no need to dismiss, criticise, ridicule, scoff or annihilate another person's viewpoint. On the contrary, they are respectful of self and of others.

The profiles outlined below are merely suggestions of what might be going on. It is always far more reliable to listen to each person's unique story. I am reluctant to spell these out because I do not want to give any notion that there is such a phenomenon as a 'personality type'. These labels are not people, not a way of judging individuals, but amazing manifestations of the difficulties in being real and true. Neither do I want people to feel they are in any way trapped into being a particular way. On the contrary, I believe we change all the time; I may be the 'carer' with one person, the 'charmer' with another and the 'intellectual' with colleagues. We are too powerful to be hedged in by any classification. However, it is true to say that we will not let go of the shadow selves that have served us so well until the time and circumstances are right. Letting go of the shadow selves does not necessarily mean a total letting go of all aspects of our protective way of relating, but it does mean being free of the compulsion to be a certain way. For example, a person who defines herself as 'a carer' may not want to give up her wonderful capacity to give, but does need to free herself to be able to receive from others also, so that the balance of give and take is present.

The most common shadow selves are the perfectionist, the carer, the taker, the rebel and the intellectual, and these are examined in more detail below. Shadow personas reveal themselves at surface and deep levels. At the surface level a person's everyday behaviour provides a window into the deeper and more hidden aspects of the shadow self.

THE 'PERFECTIONIST'

The perfectionist fears failure, is performance-driven, highly stressed, critical and intolerant of others who do not measure up to their standards, irritable and aggressive and appears insensitive to the needs of others. When confronted, perfectionists become defensive, cry or withdraw from company. They are competitive in everything they do and will avoid activities in which they do not expect to excel. They can feel easily threatened when their superior position is in jeopardy through the excellence of a competitor.

They live in the future and the past, missing out on the joys of the present. They have an overwhelming need to be in control and are generally fastidious with their belongings — tidying cushions, straightening paintings. They are systematic and become very annoyed when something is not put back in its right place.

They 'go by the book' and tend to pigeonhole people and objects. They do not cope well with change. They find it difficult to relax for fear of missing out on opportunities for greater success; they are always busy. Their minds are rarely quiet and they have no tolerance of having to wait for anything.

The perfectionist is likely to have been reared in a family where success was prized and love was conditional on success. 'To be perfect' became the protective driving force to offset rejection.

Those who present a perfectionist front to the world require considerable support and affirmation to realise that they are perfect in their essence, and it is not their actions but their unique presence that makes them worthy of love.

THE 'CARER'

Carers establish an identity of being there for others. They are thoughtful, constantly on the look-out for the needs of others. They exhaust themselves for others, constantly allowing themselves to be at the beck and call of anybody who requires help.

They rarely take to the bed when ill, and even when they are unwell they will rise from their sick bed to care for others. They ask nothing for themselves, other than being allowed to be there for others.

'No' is a word not found in their vocabulary. Their security lies in their caring role. Any attempt by another to refuse their help may result in sulking, withdrawal or 'martyr' responses. Cynicism and sarcasm may also be employed to restore the status quo of their caring role. It can be more difficult to take a caring behaviour away from somebody addicted to caring than to take a drink away from an alcoholic.

They rarely consider themselves; indeed great neglect of their personal welfare is often evident in their pursuit of the care of others. People who see themselves as carers have huge difficulty in receiving love, kindness, regard or gifts from others. Subconsciously they protectively feel unworthy to receive anything for themselves.

They subconsciously control relationships through doing everything for those close to them and are in denial of the helplessness they contribute to in others. They feel their worth lies in their caring actions and they do not allow themselves to consider that their worth and value lies within themselves.

Tiredness, burnout and fatigue syndrome are common among carers.

The carer is likely to have had a parent who modelled only being there for others and who met any protest against such 'selflessness' with labels of 'selfish', 'uncaring', 'bad'. The carer may also have come from a home where he or she cleverly learned how to please an over-demanding, aggressive and unpredictable parent. Those who are addicted to caring are not able to see that their compulsion to care is, paradoxically, an extremely selfish behaviour. It is selfish because it is controlling; it creates helplessness and blocks the receiver from saying 'no' to the care.

Like the perfectionist, those who have evolved the protective self of 'carer' need patience, love, encouragement and support to realise that their true value lies in their sacred self and not in caring actions. At a deep level the 'carer' has a strong desire to be able to ask for and to receive love.

THE 'TAKER'

The person who develops the 'taker' shadow self is opposite in all ways to the carer.

Takers' needs have to be met by others. They can be over-demanding and aggressive in the expression of their needs. Delayed gratification is not in their behavioural repertoire. They are intolerant and dismissive of those who suggest they meet their own needs.

They can sulk, throw scenes and even become violent when their needs are not met. Subconsciously they see the fulfilment of their needs by others as evidence of being loved, but sadly this is a bottomless pit as any failure in responsiveness will plunge them into the conviction that they are not loved or wanted. Individuals who are masters at getting their needs met seldom, if ever, consider the needs of others. In ingenious ways they always manage to steer the attention back to themselves.

They do not show concern for others. 'Out of sight, out of mind' aptly describes their attitude to others. They are highly dependent and do not tend to survive the death of the partner or parent who continually looked after them. Indeed, they often die before the person who was their 'carer', even though it might have been the latter who became ill first.

They tend to come from families where they had a mother who spoilt them and a father who also protected himself by being the 'taker'. Generally speaking, takers do not have good relationships with their fathers. Sadly, they remain tied to their mother's 'caring' apron strings.

Individuals who have cleverly adopted the 'taker' persona

have locked inside of themselves the drive to love and to be kind to others. They require much reassurance that in extricating themselves from their compulsion to take, their 'carers' will not abandon them, and if they do that they can learn to be there for themselves. Support from others who are in a place of freedom to give and receive love helps their freedom flight.

THE 'REBEL'

Individuals who adopt the 'rebel' persona are in a constant state of reaction to people and situations. Rebels are aggressive, critical, explosive, argumentative. They have nothing good to say about anybody or anything. They tend to have very troubled relationships and often go from one relationship to another seeking the ever elusive security so much wanted.

They are convinced that people want to exploit them and consequently are always suspicious of other people's motivations.

They tend to be competitive in work, games and social situations. Rebels may consider themselves non-conformist but rarely have any strong and developed views of their own. It is as if all their energy is expended in defending themselves against the enemy out there.

Their leadership style tends to be domineering and aggressive, and cynicism and sarcasm may be finely tuned defensive weapons.

They are not good listeners but become very angry when not listened to. They are demanding of attention and perceive any falling short in the meeting of their needs as rejection. Their response to perceived neglect can be over-the-top and devastating to the person targeted. In the typical family background of the rebel, the father or mother was hyper-critical and had high expectations of their children and themselves.

Inside the rebel feels lonely, lost, frightened and scared of rejection. However, the rebel does not show any of these vulnerabilities to others but maintains a 'brave' front.

Rebels need unconditional acceptance, a recognition of their uniqueness, an acceptance of their difference, and encouragement and support to reveal their inner feelings of hurt, fear and a sense of being unlovable.

THE 'INTELLECTUAL'

The 'intellectuals' live in their heads; they are happiest with ideas, thoughts and philosophy and are highly threatened by feelings. For protective purposes they have cleverly severed their hearts from their heads. They can appear cold and uninvolved. It seems that they do not know how to love anyone, including themselves. Any mention of the 'love' word will be quickly and critically dismissed. They can be a master of the 'cutting word', cynicism and sarcasm.

They tend to be successful in their careers but a disaster when it comes to maintaining relationships, friendships, marriage and family. Their connection with their family of origin is unemotional. They do experience an intellectual connection. The intellectual subconsciously learned the danger around emotions and conformity to the high academic expectations. More than likely both parents were addicted to academic success and possibly were not comfortable with emotional expression and receptivity. The emphasis would certainly have been on intellectual prowess.

Intellectuals tend to do very well in school, but could have been the victims of bullying. They could have been taunted by nicknames of 'professor' or 'swot' or 'teacher's pet' or 'headcase'. It is likely they could have had one close friend — a fellow intellectual — but there would be a danger of the friendship being threatened by competitiveness. All in all, intellectuals would be happiest on their own with their computer or books.

In fields of endeavour, 'intellectuals' are a minefield of knowledge and can be fascinating to listen to. However, the absence of emotion, excitement, spontaneity, thrill and love eventually causes other people to lose interest in seeking them out. Sadly, they will not allow people's withdrawal from them to dent their intellectual armour and will greet their departure with 'who needs people' or 'glad to get rid of that bore'. Of course intellectual superiority is part and parcel of this person's defensive profile.

Tragedies do not penetrate their barriers around feelings and this can appear quite shocking to others who allow themselves to feel rage, grief and loss.

It is very difficult to persuade the 'intellectual' to go for help to explore the vast and wonderful emotional world that lies so well hidden. A precipitant to seeking help can be a physical health problem such as high blood pressure, heart disease, cancer or migraine headaches. It takes considerable pressure and strain to hold back the tidal wave of feelings that is present and, eventually, this takes its toll with expression in physical illness.

Considerable patience is needed for those 'who live in and through their heads' to help and encourage them to mend the line between their head and heart.

PART THREE
TOTAL ECLIPSE OF THE SELF

CHAPTER SEVEN
INVISIBLE SELF

TOTAL ECLIPSE OF THE SELF

Is there anything more painful than not feeling loved, wanted, valued, seen and cherished by others in this world? There is — to be in the darkest place of not loving yourself. 'Total eclipse' is a way of describing a person who possesses no sense of self. 'Partial eclipse' is where a person maintains some sense of his or her real self.

Over the years I have encountered individuals who have described themselves as 'worthless', 'nothing', 'shit', 'despicable', 'invisible', 'disgusting', 'horrible', 'hateful', 'dirt'. These labels describe the conscious shadow self they present to the world. The subconscious fear underlying the invisible self is to show even the slightest sign that they are of any value and somebody worth loving. Within relationships and cultures where great neglect exists, deep and sometimes terrible protections are called upon to guard the light of self.

Unconsciously you recognise how extremely dangerous it is to be truly oneself, while at the same time your protectors act as powerful messages alerting others to the dark place in which you live. Examples of protectors against great neglect are:

□ alcohol abuse
□ addiction to money/ work
□ anorexia
□ bulimia

□ chronic anxiety
□ delusions
□ depression
□ dropping-out from responsible living

- drug abuse
- fanaticism
- hallucinating
- hatred of others; hatred of self
- extreme jealousy
- masochism; sado-masochism
- lack of ambition
- obsessive-compulsive behaviour
- paranoia
- possessiveness
- rage
- self-mutilation
- serious illness
- intense mental torment
- violence
- isolation

THE HISTORY BEHIND INVISIBILITY

The darkness of a person's family or other surrounding cultures have led that individual to totally hide the light of their unique presence. The family culture may have been physically caring but emotionless or actively neglectful (persistent emotional, sexual and physical trauma) or symbiotic (no expression of individuality allowed). These family situations are where parents, who themselves had no hint of their sacredness, bring children into their dark world, and the cycle of neglect is repeated. When the wider cultures of school, extended family, community and country do not intervene in such neglectful familial circumstances, they contribute greatly to the darkness felt by members of such families. The wider cultures have a responsibility to ensure that children living in the absence of light be given lifelines. The parents are the obvious target for intervention but the children need to experience their presence being cherished by as many people as possible outside their unhappy homes. Turning a blind eye and rationalising that it is the responsibility of parents to look after their children are protective mechanisms that do not serve the children, the parents and society. Within the major constraints of their deeply shadowed worlds, the parents are doing their best. They need all the help they can get, but intervention must rest on understanding and compassion and not on judgment.

Individuals who feel invisible unconsciously know how they need to live their lives, but they also know too well the major threats to self that exist should they attempt being real. The histories of these persons make grim reading; invisibility makes total sense when you know their stories.

The source and meaning of any of the above signs of invisibility are unique to the individual. To cluster symptoms under a label such as 'depressive', 'schizophrenic' or 'neurotic' is to further darken the presence of the person exhibiting these responses.

The possible hidden challenges (given in parentheses) to the following protectors are

- alcohol or drug addicted (express how you feel)
- ashamed of self (express how much you count)
- blaming (be responsible for self)
- cannot take compliments (be open to receiving positive feedback)
- continually miserable (embrace self and life)
- cynical and sarcastic (say what you really feel and think)
- deeply troubled relationships (be independent)
- delusional (be real)
- denial of vulnerabilities (acceptance and expression of vulnerabilities)
- depressed (live your own life)
- drop-out from responsible living (face reality)
- emotionless (expressive and receptive to all emotions)
- extremely perfectionistic (embrace failure)
- extremely critical of self (know you are not your behaviour)

- ☐ feels everybody else is better off (live your own life)
- ☐ hypersensitive to criticism (listen to your own intuitive voice)
- ☐ masochism; sado-masochism (express the pain you dare not express)
- ☐ lack of ambition (embrace the adventure of life)
- ☐ obsessive-compulsive behaviour (know that you are not your behaviour)
- ☐ paranoid (trust your own intuition)
- ☐ possessive of others (possess self)
- ☐ rage (take responsibility for your actions)
- ☐ hostile, lonely and isolated (reach out to others)
- ☐ indecisive (risk-take)
- ☐ living in a fantasy world (discover the reality of your own worth)
- ☐ living totally through others (live life from the inside out)
- ☐ neglectful of self (take care of self)
- ☐ pessimistic and fatalistic (be realistic)
- ☐ reacts badly to criticism (talk about hidden hurts)
- ☐ rigid and inflexible (tolerate difference)
- ☐ suicidal (break the silence on hidden neglect)
- ☐ hates self (love self)
- ☐ highly anxious (approve of self)
- ☐ volatile (find the solid ground of your own sacred interiority)
- ☐ vindictive (take responsibility for your own feelings of hurt)

WHAT LIES BEHIND INVISIBILITY IS CONSTANTLY BEING REVEALED

The real self is forever pushing to create the situation where it can do without the shadow persona it has had to build around self. The need to love, to be loved, to be spontaneous, free, creative, individual and different constantly reveals itself, but in a hidden way that maintains the protection of the self from perceived threats. For example, individuals who are convinced that people are talking about them, or seeing evil in them, or listening into their conversations, or putting certain thoughts into their mind, are cleverly projecting on to others what they really want for themselves: to talk about what is troubling them, to visibly show the 'evil' that has been done to them, to have people listen to their stories and to be able to express freely, without fear, the thoughts that occupy their minds. Their subconscious hope is that others will spot the revelations of their hidden worlds and offer them the opportunities to begin the journey of real self-expression. Regrettably, because most people are in shadow themselves, and thereby are threatened by paranoid behaviours, those who are invisible tend to be shunned. Such a shadow response plunges the person who is invisible further into darkness, and the efforts to attract attention now have to be escalated. Too often the final action is suicide, arising from the despair of ever finding love, understanding and compassion.

There are those people who express their invisibility in hallucinations — 'I'm Jesus Christ' or 'I'm the Mother of God' or 'I'm possessed by the devil'. The hidden issues are symbolised in these amazing expressions of invisibility: 'I need my light to be seen', 'I need to nurture myself', and 'there are major pressures inside of me I need to talk about'.

People who display obsessive-compulsive behaviours also cleverly manifest their hidden fears. Possible suggestions of what needs to be seen are given in parentheses:

□ obsessive-compulsive checking of regulators, for example, taps, gas and electricity controls ('I dare not express how I feel')

- obsessive-compulsive checking of light ('I dare not show my light')
- obsessive-compulsive hand washing ('I dare not talk about the "dirty laundry" that needs to be washed in public')
- obsessive-compulsive tidying ('I dare not express the disorder I feel inside of myself')
- obsessive-compulsive cleaning ('I dare not talk about how I feel I've been treated like dirt')
- obsessive-compulsive counting ('I am terrified to say that I count')

Recall that the hidden messages being revealed in these symptoms will be unique to each person and the above are only possible suggestions of what needs to be seen.

When people emerge from family and other cultures terrified of being real, it is a major responsibility for individuals who are more fortunate, and for political and social systems that purport to be caring in nature, to be vigilant so that the subtle flags flown by people in darkness are not flown in vain.

SOURCES OF INVISIBILITY

The sources of invisibility lie in relationships and cultures. It is the intensity, frequency, endurance and duration of the blocks to real expression of self that lead to invisibility rather than to partial eclipse of the self.

RELATIONSHIP BLOCKS

Children born to people addicted to drugs, alcohol, work, violence or extreme passivity, suffer greatly. I have worked with adults who as infants were left alone for days without any nurturance or who were physically violated because they cried or who were sexually violated or mutilated because of drug-induced hallucinations. These experiences continued for days, weeks, years on end.

Similarly, parents who are deeply depressed or highly anxious or perfectionist or paranoid are not in a position to provide the ongoing caring, cherishing and mature direction their children need to be able to hold on to their real selves. Moodiness, irritability, dismissiveness, punishment, extreme fussiness, over-control, protection, scoldings, threats of abandonment are some of the everyday experiences of the children of these parents.

There is no intention here of judging or blaming these parents, but the reality is that the parents' own sense of invisibility is repeated in their children. As parents, teachers, husbands, wives, lovers, leaders, we can only give what we have ourselves. It is not possible for those living in darkness to bring the light of love to others. They have a responsibility *to* their own darkness before they can be effective in their relationships with others. When the opportunities are not there for them to do that, the responsibility lies with the social systems in which they live to ensure that darkness does not lead to more darkness. Whilst matters are improving in the greater care of children by community, education and government bodies, a lot more is required. For example, parenting is still not regarded as a profession and there is no requirement for any training or reflection before taking on the hardest profession of all. Neither are child-minders, teachers or community workers required to reflect on and take responsibility to their own shadow baggage before embarking on the rearing, caring and teaching of children.

CULTURAL BLOCKS

Anonymity is not an uncommon experience of individuals in family, school, classroom, religious, work and political cultures. A leading Catholic churchman said in a lecture at a Millennium conference that 'individuality had destroyed the family'. Such a claim comes from the darkest aspects of a patriarchal culture that gave no visibility to women, saw all human beings as basically evil and had the arrogance to put power only in the hands of a few 'privileged' men called to do the Church's bidding. The loss of influence is seen in the exodus from religious life and the high fall-off in church attendance. Individuality is the cornerstone of healthy cultures. Mutual respect and care flourishes in social systems where each person's difference and individuality is celebrated.

Many children and indeed teachers experience not being cherished in school systems. Some children suffered greatly at the hands of school cultures that lauded the 'bright' and castigated the 'dull'. Persistent bullying in and out of class by teachers and peers has led to some children committing suicide or murdering others. Teachers themselves have long been victims of educational systems that were not nurturing in nature.

Workplaces have long been notorious in their neglect of employees. Violence, verbal denigration, bullying and exploitation are still commonplace. Work should always be worthy of people's dignity and this is both an individual and a collective responsibility.

It is also the case that individuals who hide all aspects of their true selves can be members of a political system that shows little or no value for the individual, exploits those who are vulnerable and enforces rigid conformity to the system's dark political philosophy.

HELPING INDIVIDUALS WHO FEEL INVISIBLE

When individuals who feel they are 'nobody' come or are brought to health services, very often their symptoms are medicalised, they are psychiatrically labelled, hopeless prognoses are given and psychotropic medication is prescribed as the very limited therapeutic option. Psychiatric labelling is a subconscious reaction on the part of professionals and families to distance themselves from the extreme shadow behaviours of those who are in deep distress. In effect, medical labelling is itself a shadow behaviour and it serves the powerful purpose of protecting professionals from having to acknowledge their own helplessness; it also protects family members, particularly parents or partners, from looking at how their shadow selves are part of the reason why such distress in those labelled has come about.

I have worked with many people labelled with schizophrenia, manic-depression, bipolar depression, endogenous depression, personality disorder and attention-deficit disorder. A number of these individuals realised their worth without the adjunct of medication, others with it. All eventually let go of reliance on medication. Their stories were amazing, and though great patience is required from myself and the person seeking help, it has always been a privilege to accompany them on their journey to realising their incomparable worth, sacredness and uniqueness. What has not been recognised by many health professionals is that individuals seeking help know the answers to their plight, but, because they are rarely asked, they have kept this knowledge, albeit unconsciously, to themselves. Most people who are invisible to themselves are told what their problems are, but, in truth and in practice, the only person who has the solution to why they operate in dark ways is the person themselves. The role of the helper is to act as a mirror to reflect what is already known but as yet has not been expressed nor actualised. This is not to say that helpers only need to be trained to reflect back inner realities to those who seek their help. Clients also need professional helpers who have realised their own worth (or at least are progressing towards that goal), who possess patience, understanding and compassion, and who are able to provide informed witnessing to the events that led to their clients shutting out the light of their sacred selves. I also believe clients benefit from being put in touch with people and cultures that support their realisation process.

PART FOUR
THE EMERGENCE OF THE SELF

CHAPTER EIGHT

JOURNEY TOWARDS SELF-REALISATION

INTRODUCTION

Realising your true self is a long, complex, difficult and exciting journey. It is a *long* journey because of the distance you have travelled from your real self over the many years that you have had to hide yourself. The journey inwards is *complex* because it entails an understanding of and compassion for the shadow protectors that, while being necessary, have hidden your light. It is a *difficult* journey because it entails revealing what is hidden, and that means touching into deep hurt, pain, shame, humiliation, anger, rage, fear and terror. But the journey is also *exciting* because of the gradual discovery of the amazing expansiveness of your interior world and your sacredness, uniqueness and giftedness.

Some of the groundwork steps on the journey inwards are:

- □ Recognising what living in the light might mean.
- □ Realising you have never stopped loving yourself.
- □ Taking up the challenge of realising self.
- □ Starting the journey inwards.
- □ Realising rather than changing self.
- □ Embracing your shadow selves.
- □ Embracing what lies hidden.
- □ Embracing the shadow cast on others.

When starting on your journey inwards, the most important thing to remember is that up to this point you have guarded powerfully your sacred self. The time has come for you to go underneath your protectors and bring forward what is truly amazing — yourself.

RECOGNISING WHAT LIVING IN THE LIGHT MIGHT MEAN

There are a small number of people who really live their own lives, have a strong sense of their wonder and uniqueness, are definite in the expression of their individuality and possess an equally deep regard for the sacredness and individuality of others. Some characteristics of the person living in the light are:

- □ asks for support, help and advice when needed
- □ has capacity to give and receive love
- □ cares for environment
- □ is decisive
- □ is emotionally expressive and receptive
- □ embraces failure
- □ is flexible
- □ is free to be self
- □ honours difference in self and others
- □ is independent
- □ listens to self and others
- □ loves challenge
- □ loves privacy
- □ is non-conformist
- □ is open
- □ is optimistic
- □ is physically healthy
- □ reaches out to self, others and life with mind and heart
- □ respects self and others
- □ sees failure and success as relative terms

- ☐ has sense of self separate from all behaviour
- ☐ stays separate from the behaviour of others
- ☐ is spiritual
- ☐ is spontaneous
- ☐ takes responsibility for own life
- ☐ is wholeheartedly involved in life

Even people who are true to themselves need protective behaviours when faced with people or cultures that do not respect their presence. In the face of such threats it is wise to retreat and take care of your sacred self until such time as it is safe to express it. Retreating is not, of course, the only option; another possibility is to become involved in sub-cultural movements that assert the rights of people and provide opportunities for those in darkness to come into the light. For example, the women's movement has advanced hugely the presence of women in what were predominantly patriarchal societies. Parent groups have also increased their voice in society and children have gained more visibility, certainly in Western society.

People who live in the light have either been fortunate in being unconditionally cherished when children and allowed to express their individuality in a multiplicity of ways, or as adults they have had opportunities to take the road less travelled and return to the fullness of their being. There have always been people who live in the light: perhaps it was religion/spirituality that gave them the opportunity to do so, at least up until recently; now there are further opport-unities through therapy and greater access to different spiritual teachings. However, there are many people who are 'stuck' in the darkness of their past experiences and the cultures that demeaned their presence. Patience and com-passion are required if there is to be any hope of those who are in shadow seeking the light.

REALISING YOU HAVE NEVER STOPPED LOVING YOURSELF

The notion that the self never ceases to take care of itself may seem preposterous when you look at the number of people who are miserable, anxious, depressed, lonely, sick, driven, sadistic and violent. If you think of the self as a unique pearl of immense value, then the lengths you go to in order to protect that self become clearer. Many people will want the precious pearl, may even kill to get it, and so it needs safeguarding against all sorts of perils – robbery, threats, blackmail, violence. In order to hold on to your precious pearl, you will put it in an impenetrable safe, avail of a sophisticated security system, insure the pearl against theft or damage, carry a weapon and do anything else necessary to make your treasure safe. All of these defence behaviours guarantee the safety of the pearl. In the same way, you create the most amazing defences to protect your unique self. Compared to the precious pearl, the dangers that your sacred self faces are multiple and far more threatening – physical, emotional, social, intellectual, sexual, occupational, behavioural and spiritual. In the same way that the pearl in the safe has been untouched, so too the self that is hidden behind defensive walls – no matter how high or deep – remains intact, untouched, perfect.

TAKING UP THE CHALLENGE OF REALISING SELF

Being real is a fearful prospect to people in shadow, and the greater the shadow the greater the fear. People in shadow know full well the dangers of authenticity, and it seems safer to stay within the relative comfort of being hidden. But in the words of D.W. Winnicott, a leading psychoanalyst: 'It may be a joy to be hidden but it is a disaster not to be found.' The prospect of making a U (you) turn and going on the road less travelled, back to your real self, can lead to an increase in protective forces. People in shadow know that being real may initially lead to greater insecurity, vulnerability and confusion. Take the example of the woman making a decision to leave an unfulfilling and neglectful relationship. This is no easy step, considering the risk of going it alone, maybe for the first time, the enmeshment of the families of the partners, the unresolved marital conflict, the threats of breakdown, suicide, aggression or apathy on the part of the partner who wants to hold on to the marriage and the very difficult question of what happens to the children. Relatives and friends may be discouraging and parents unsupportive. In such circumstances the individual may cleverly procrastinate to avoid the threats that are present.

Others who are fearful of being true to self may present as 'too busy' to change, talk endlessly about all they have to do and deflect any attempt to steer them on to the subject of self-realisation by bringing up some 'urgent' issue or insisting that it is time to go. These people can create the illusion that they are always taking on challenges, but the challenges tend to be all external projects — new kitchen, new car, wonderfully redesigned garden, new job, fresh interests — and the call to the inner world of self, independence and expression of real self is cleverly avoided.

An equally ingenious strategy for the person frightened of the journey of self-realisation is apathy — it is just too much trouble to move forward. Another strategy for avoiding the emergence of self is to blame others for their lack of support and encouragement: 'If only my friends would say "go for it"', or 'If only I was sure my family would support me.' Yet another common response to the fear of forward movement is to set goals too high so that failure occurs, allowing the resigned response: 'I knew there was no point to this self-development stuff.'

Fear of failure is endemic in society and is usefully employed when the challenge to be real arises. 'What if things don't work out?'; 'What if I lose my friends?'; 'What guarantees can you give me?'

Realising self is by no means easy but, in the long run, not being authentic carries far more risks. If you do not respond to the early signals that your presence is darkened, the psyche may need to resort to physical disease or deep emotional distress to wake you up to finding the help and support required to redeem your hidden self.

Some individuals may make a break for freedom from, for instance, a neglectful workplace, an unhappy marriage or an oppressive family, only to return after a short time. Inevitably, they will find the pressures have not changed, and their next attempt is likely to be far more determined. During times of challenge, it is to be expected that you will return to old protective patterns of behaviour, until more solid ground is found for the movement inwards.

Your wisdom and strength are always there – they created your shadow worlds to protect you and are equally there to enable you on your journey back to the light. It helps enormously to be surrounded by people who love you 'for yourself', who give you heart to go on, who believe in you and provide support when needed. Such supportive figures may not be members of your family, nor work colleagues, nor old friends who, on the contrary, may be the very ones from whom you had to hide your real self.

It is those who are in shadow themselves who ultimately

hold the power to free themselves from the hidden world. Other people and the places where they live, work, recreate and pray can be supportive, but it is the person in hiding who has to take the steps of coming out from behind their defences.

Touching into your real self often triggers challenges in your external world as well — new friends, new interests, healthy eating, new job, different taste in reading, new home décor, new wardrobe. All of these changes may be reflective, supportive and reinforcing of the inner changes you have made. No matter where you are in your journey, patience, frequency, intensity and endurance of your efforts to be yourself are what are especially needed for you to achieve the fruits of your labours — your sacred self.

STARTING THE JOURNEY INWARDS

Your shadow self does not reflect the true shape of your uniqueness and individuality; what it does do is cleverly mask it to a high or low degree, depending on the frequency, intensity, endurance and duration of the experienced threats. The shadow self is not a static screen — it moves to reveal some aspects of your real self when threats are not present. However, when individuals have experienced great neglect of their sacred presence, the shadow self tends to be rigid and inflexible.

However simplistic it may sound, the truth is that being true to your own self is created by unconditionally loving yourself. It is not that you do not know how vital are love of self and freedom to express self, but there are potent forces about us that make this journey inwards a very threatening prospect. To travel inwards you need to take account of your shadow selves and the dark aspects of your relationships and places in which you live, play and work.

When individuals are heavily in shadow and experience few or no glimpses of their real selves, they need professional help to enter into and go through their shadow worlds so they can eventually emerge into their light. It is essential that these people feel loved, safe and secure with their helper; otherwise little progress is likely to occur. At times, they may project their deep terror onto their helper and consequently see the helper as the parent or other adult who neglected them, but once the helper stays unconditionally loving and does not personalise the client's projections, then movement will occur, albeit slowly, in the direction of the light.

For individuals who do experience some contact with their true selves — however fleeting — and who have people who are supportive of their inner journey, what follows in this chapter and the following one in terms of realising their selves will help in accelerating that long and exciting journey inwards.

REALISING RATHER THAN CHANGING SELF

The realisation of self does not involve changing any aspect of yourself or your behaviour. Your protective behaviours have been developed for a sound and sacred purpose, and it is a shadow behaviour to attempt to eliminate them directly. Your shadow self is not the target for change — this has served you well — embrace it. Your challenge lies in realising, bringing forward, and expressing what has lain hidden for so long; not changing but emerging; in so doing, automatically, without intervention, the protective behaviours will begin to reduce and eventually disappear. When you begin to express what has been hidden, the light of your real self shines out and radiates into your shadow world, thereby slowly but surely dissipating the darkness. It is the light that creates the darkness and it is the light that dissipates it.

When you come into the fullness of your being and the possession of the full breadth of human qualities (masculine and feminine), then the shadow responses of oppression, control, lessening, belittling, dismissiveness, rejection, violence, passivity, fear, timidity need no longer be part of your behavioural repertoire. Those responses belong to your shadow world. In the domain of the light of your real self, what emerges is loving kindness, unconditionality, fairness, justice, compassion and understanding, assertiveness, sureness and a solidity that nothing can rock.

EMBRACING YOUR SHADOW SELF

The purpose of the journey inwards is not only to discover your real self, but also to appreciate the power of your shadow self. The appreciation of the strength and creativity of your shadow self goes a long way towards taking up the challenge of embracing your shadow self. Your shadow self is your friend, your ally. It has served you well in a world that did not properly affirm your presence. Not only has your shadow self protected you from further blows to your presence, it also continually presents you with the precise challenges that you need to take on in order to come more fully into your presence. It is you who determines what these challenges are, since your journey inwards is unique to your biographical history.

One of the first milestones on the path to realising self is acknowledging how well the conscious side of your shadow self has served you. Individuals who hate their aggression, depression, anxiety, shyness or timidity are not yet ready to begin the journey home to themselves. Embarrassment, criticism and rejection of your conscious shadow behaviours are further defences against threats to self that still abound, and are also defences against taking on the challenge of being real. Support from outside yourself (friend, partner, colleague, writer, medical practitioner, counsellor, psychologist) may be required for you to come to a place of embracing your shadow self.

Embracing your shadow self involves bearing witness to all the neglectful experiences you have endured and honouring the protectors devised to reduce those threats to the expression of yourself. A further requirement is taking responsibility *for* the blocks to the presence of others that emerged from your place of shadow. There is no room for blame, but there is room for the honest expression of deep regret that you were not able to cherish the sacred presence of another. Such honesty touches the heart of the person who was at the receiving end of your shadow behaviour, it equalises the relationship and it offers the other person the opportunity to be true to their life experiences.

It is a useful exercise to chart the road that took you away from your real self. On the map you can list those individuals, experiences and aspects of the cultures that you inhabited that blocked (or facilitated) your being true to yourself. Remember, for the majority of people it was not all doom and gloom.

EMBRACING WHAT LIES HIDDEN

Behind every conscious shadow behaviour is hidden what you dare not express about yourself. Getting to this secret world is essential to the realisation of yourself. The discoveries you make of what you have been forced to hide of yourself will be unique to you. In my own case the hidden issues I eventually detected were:

- Don't ask anything for myself.
- Don't look for love.
- Don't affirm my own special physical presence.
- Don't think for myself.
- Don't celebrate sexuality.
- Don't fail.
- Don't have my own beliefs.
- Don't be too different.
- Don't say 'no' to people who have needs of me.

The shadow identities I had for myself were:

- 'Carer'
- 'Rescuer'
- 'Loner'
- 'Good person'
- 'Unattractive person'

These personas were clever constructions to ensure that I did not engage in behaviours that would run contrary to what I expected of myself and what others expected of me. The contrary dare-not-do actions were:

- to think well of myself
- to assert that I counted
- to ask for help and support
- to reach out for intimacy and friendship
- to express the 'bad' thoughts and feelings that were part of me as much as the 'good' parts
- to express my own physical attractiveness

Clearly, bringing into the open what has been hidden is easier said than done; otherwise you would have been

authentic long before now. An assessment of what circumstances and which people represent the greatest threats to
the expression of what lies hidden is a powerful step on the
journey inwards. Maybe the block is a parent on whom you
are still dependent for acceptance and whose expectations
you are terrified of not fulfilling. Getting support and help to
cut the ties that bind you to this parent, who is in deep
shadow, is a way forward. Acceptance of yourself and the
self-permission to live your own life are further stepping
stones for you to express truly who you are.

The block to real expression may be the culture in which you
work, live, pray or play. The challenge is to find cultures that
are worthy of your dignity. Such places exist and provide the
platform for you to depart from social systems that darken
your presence.

EMBRACING THE SHADOW YOU CAST ON OTHERS

The shadow you cast on others is a projection outwards of
the hidden parts of yourself, and this mirrors opportunities
for you to be real to yourself and others. Typically what you
judge or condemn in others is what lies hidden within
yourself. When you own your projections, you begin the
process of realising self and affirming the unique and sacred
presence of others.

Seeing the dark reality of what you project onto others is
daunting but enriching. Judgments reflect hidden parts of
self: some examples of judgments with accompanying
possible hidden messages are given below. When you take on
the challenge of the hidden issues, automatically your
shadow tendency to judge others will begin to decrease: the
light of authenticity dispels the darkness of projection.

JUDGMENT	POSSIBLE HIDDEN MESSAGE
□ 'You're so selfish.'	□ 'I need to be responsible for myself.'
□ 'You're always late.'	□ 'I don't give time to myself.'
□ 'You're a bastard.'	□ 'I don't take care of myself.'
□ 'You're so intelligent.'	□ 'I'm afraid to show my cleverness.'
□ 'You're such a carer.'	□ 'I'm afraid to care for others.'
□ 'You're an alcoholic.'	□ 'I'm afraid to express that I need more in the relationship.'
□ 'You piss me off.'	□ 'I don't dare express my real needs.'

CHAPTER NINE
REALISING SELF

INTRODUCTION

Having established an understanding, acceptance and responsibility for your shadow behaviours, you are ready to proceed further down the inner road towards realisation of self. Action is the key, and the active focus needs to be on what lies hidden — those aspects of yourself you dare not show. It is the bringing to light of those hidden parts of self where the true challenge of self-realisation lies. Accessing those hidden aspects can be done through identifying your shadow behaviours and personas and then determining the opposite of what you show — this is what lies hidden. This active process involves:

- Being mindful of self.
- Being real with self and others.
- Affirming self and others.
- Realising your presence — physical, sexual, emotional, intellectual, behavioural, social, creative and spiritual.
- Listening to your own inner voice.
- Realising the expansiveness of being yourself.
- Confronting people who darken your presence.
- Confronting cultures that darken your presence.
- Staying separate from the shadow behaviours of others.
- Finding support for realising self.

BEING MINDFUL OF SELF

Each person has a unique presence, and being mindful means staying in touch with your own presence and the real presence of others. It also means 'minding' yourself and others. The latter type of minding is practising loving kindness towards yourself and others. The former kind of mindfulness is about seeing behind your shadow persona and acknowledging your hidden sacred person; you can do exactly the same for others. In your mindfulness practice, be sure that no matter where you are and whom you are with, you hold onto possession of your unique presence and you are mindful of the special presence of others.

Below is an affirmation exercise on the sacredness of self that you can either read silently to yourself or have another read to you, or tape your own voicing of it and use the tape to practise. The morning time before you begin your active day is a good time to practise and also when you finish your day's work. It is a particularly good exercise when you feel you have lost touch with yourself.

MY SACRED SELF

There is a deeper part of me that knows who I am, that knows that:

I am sacred.

I am intuitive.

I am powerful beyond measure.

I am unique.

I am gifted.

I possess vast intellect.

I am different.

I can love.

I can receive love.

I am creative.

I am part of an infinite universe.

Somehow along the way of life some or all aspects of my unique light have had to be hidden. My wise self has guarded the precious light of my being in the darkness of shadow selves, false personas that hide my real presence and darken the presence of others. I now know that I would not have survived without hiding who I really am. I am ready to let go of the protection of dependence on others and of being a passive member of dark cultures. I realise my amazing self and see the unique light of others hidden behind their shadow selves.

There will be many voices that will shout their 'bad' advice, cry to me 'to mend their lives', and do all in their shadow power to keep me in darkness. For my sake and their sakes I can no longer listen to their shadow voice. I need to find and listen to my own inner voice that will guide and keep me company as I stride deeper and deeper into the vast interiority of my real self. I will seek the company and support of those who are light-giving to help me stay on the road less travelled.

All the time on the journey, I know that the amazing power that has guarded my sacredness all these past years is now there to open my mind and heart to fully seeing and expressing who I really am.

Dependence, fear, judgment, avoidance, timidity, depression, passivity and competitiveness will no longer be my bedfellows. Spontaneity, freedom, independence, eagerness to learn, empathy, compassion, excitement, challenge, creativity, unconditional love of myself and others, intuition, authenticity, patience and exploration of my inner and outer worlds are my new and powerful ways of being in the world.

I know that there are difficult decisions to be made when I encounter individuals and cultures that darken my presence and the presence of others. I know that when I protectively sell myself out of a need to belong, I ultimately buy a life of misery. In such conformity I am neither a friend to myself nor to others. I know I have a sacred responsibility to belong to myself, to be real and authentic and not wait for others to transform themselves.

My hope is that as the light of my sacred self shines forth, it will touch the minds and hearts of those people and cultures that are in darkness. I know that I can only save my own life but that others have the immense power to do likewise. I do know that as I am liberated from my shadow self, my presence provides support for others to liberate themselves.

I was born to manifest the uniqueness, wonder, sacredness and glory of my being. I know that all these words do not create but reflect who I really am. This is the beginning of my re-birthing, of my realising my sacred self.

BEING REAL WITH SELF AND OTHERS

Joy in self is not about continual happiness but about being in touch with what is happening inside and outside of ourselves. Most pain comes from being hard on ourselves or denying certain feelings. If we practise friendliness towards all of those experiences and honestly work from a place of acceptance of their purpose, then mature progress will be maintained. For example, when you have jealous thoughts and feelings, kindly accepting their presence will bring you to see what they reveal to you about the absence of your own valuing of your sacred presence and the challenge to return to possession of your real self. When the latter happens, there will be no need for you to compare yourself to everybody else.

Similarly, when another person experiences protective feelings, thoughts or actions, it is loving kindness to acknowledge what is happening to them, but also to communicate what is happening to you in response to their behaviour. For example, if a friend is being aggressive, you might say 'I accept you're feeling very strongly about this issue but I'm feeling threatened and I do not feel safe enough to honestly respond to you or even to stay in your presence.' Should this response not de-escalate the aggression, then you may need to leave the threatening situation. Similarly, when someone expresses terror of having a life-threatening illness, your mindful response is to actively listen, acknowledge what has been revealed and, if you are feeling helpless in response to what is being said, to admit to it. Such honesty will make it safer for the other person to go deeper into what is happening for him or her.

AFFIRMING SELF AND OTHERS

To affirm is to state what is real and enduring about self; more often than not it is acknowledging those parts of yourself that up to this point in time you dared not express to yourself or others. Affirmation has absolutely nothing to do with behaviours but everything to do with person. Some examples of affirmations are given below, but find your own language for expressing the truth about yourself. It is useful to have a few key affirmations that resonate strongly with you and that you can employ readily, not only in times of crisis but regularly throughout your day.

Affirmations

'I love myself and others unconditionally, both in the giving and receiving.'

'I am determined to live my own life in accordance with my own inner voice.'

'I am unique, sacred and special.'

'I will be true to myself.'

'I will only do what is worthy of my dignity.'

'I respect and value my needs and the needs of others in any relationship and will act accordingly.'

'I take full responsibility and allow others to take total responsibility for thoughts, feelings, dreams and actions.'

REALISING YOUR PRESENCE

Realising your presence is about discovering that solid ground of your expansiveness and power as a unique human being — that sure place from which nobody or no social system can belittle, exclude or exile you. You need to touch into all the ways of expressing your being: physical, sexual, emotional, intellectual, behavioural, social, creative and spiritual. Touching into what you are is not accomplished through intellectualising or positive thinking, but by allowing mind and heart to see, acknowledge and express your power beyond measure. It is primarily a process of being, rather than doing. It is allowing what has always been there to rise to the surface, and as it appears, to greet the emergence of the light with loving kindness, joy, celebration and a determination to stay present to it. As an adult, it is only you yourself who can realise your presence. Without your commitment to being present to your real self, no amount of work on the part of another to help you to move inwards is likely to be helpful. Support from others helps the process of going on the road less travelled, but only you can open the door and allow in that belief in you and support of you.

No two people are the same and no two people express all the different aspects of self in the same way. In spite of major pressures to conform, each member of a social system finds a way to be different from all other members. Difference is a wonderful expression of the uniqueness of each human being, and when it is celebrated, individuals do not have to go to the extremes of distressing, disruptive or bizarre behaviours in order to be seen and heard.

Here and now, as an adult, no longer having to depend on others, you can give yourself permission to express your difference through all the channels available to you. What is important is that such expression be from the inside out rather than from the outside in. Up to now you took your cues of how to be from others in order to survive individuals and social systems that controlled and demeaned you. As one of my clients so succinctly put it: 'I lived in other people's skins; it's time I learned to live in my own skin.'

When you express yourself from your own interiority, the various aspects of your presence emerge in a quiet, calm, yet definite way. There is no drive to prove yourself to others or to get through to them about any aspect of yourself. On the contrary, the only person you wish to convince of your sacredness is yourself. You see that communication is not about getting through to others but about getting through to yourself.

REALISING YOUR PHYSICAL PRESENCE

There is no other physical presence like you; your body is a unique expression of your special and unrepeatable person. Not only is your body *uniquely beautiful*, it is also *always right*. Every pain, ache, unpleasant symptom, as well as every physical feeling of fitness, energy and well-being are always right. *Your body is your ally*; it continually feeds back to you how much of your real presence is hidden or revealed.

When you listen to your body and respond to its messages, you are well on the way to realising self.

Back pain, headaches, overweight, underweight, stomach pain, chest pains, illnesses are all revelations of your shadow self. When you respond to physical symptoms with attention, care and nurturance, you automatically touch into your being. Furthermore, when you acknowledge the physical neglect that exists in the social systems of which you are a member and make the difficult decisions that may sometimes be called for, you are expressing your realness. Confronting neglect is an act of love, and it is that action that brings you back to your light.

What would help the realisation of your physical presence is to list the neglectful experiences of the past, the labels others put on your body, the descriptions you yourself carry, and your daily neglect of your body — for example, rushing, racing, missing meals, over-eating, lack of rest. All of these shadow behaviours present the opportunities for you to do the opposite, and thereby treat your body with the loving kindness it deserves.

Quiet, heart-driven rehearsal of affirmations that reflect your physical uniqueness and rightness may help your physical realisation of self.

'My body is special.'
'There is no other physical presence like mine in the world.'
'I want to love and care for my body.'
'My body is always right.'
'My body is my ally.'
'My body is sacred.'
'I want to enjoy the pleasures my body provides.'

Feel your energy, feel the support of your body, let your body be loose and relaxed, breathe deeply from your diaphragm and notice the steady, comfortable rhythm when you breathe normally. Feel the power in your arms and chest and let your feet be solid on the ground. Listen to your body's need for comfort, food, water, rest, exercise and sleep. At all times treat it with loving kindness. Regular moderate physical exercise, the practice of deep relaxation methods, diaphragmatic breathing, healthy diet and balanced lifestyle give life to the realising of your physical presence.

REALISING YOUR SEXUAL PRESENCE

Sexuality is a vital source of energy that has no necessary connection with sexual activity. It is a wellspring within you, a spiritual and emotional resource within your body. Religions have done harm to sexual being and expression more than any other social system. The rejection of sexuality has created a shadow world where individuals have had to develop protective ways of meeting their sexual needs. In the shadow world of sexual expression, the 'being' of sexuality has been lost. Clearly, any sexual violations (uninvited sexual intimacy) lead to individuals hiding their sexual presence or totally devaluing or repressing it.

Sexuality is an important aspect of self-realisation. There has been a huge cultural barrier to talking openly about sexuality, and breaking this barrier of silence is the first step to realising your sexual presence.

The challenge for men in realising their sexual expression is to learn to be intimate: the line between the penis and the heart needs to be reconnected. Men need to embrace their vulnerability and give expression to what they are feeling: it is not just a question of learning to cry, but also expressing tenderness, compassion and kindness.

The challenge for each woman is to affirm her fundamental sense of beauty and worth in her own right. This realisation of your unique beauty is not something that you can earn from the outside; it has to come from the inside.

Loving and caring for our bodies is fundamental to the realisation of our sexual presence. Caring for our bodies involves regular exercise for fitness but also for pleasure, breathing deeply, stretching your body fully, healthy eating, hygiene, enjoying a long bath and reading about your body. Sexual time with self is looking in the mirror with pride, sensual and sexual massage and fantasy time. Sexual time with another is asking for what you want, enjoying closeness with another, saying no when you want to, saying what brings you joy, saying when it hurts, crying when you need to and having fun. Realising your sexual presence also includes objecting to any verbal or non-verbal behaviour that ridicules men or women, lessens the sacredness of sexuality and is exploitative of sexual vulnerability.

Each one of us has a unique biographical history, and what lies hidden in terms of our sexuality is individual to each of us. Make a list of the protective ways you manage your sexuality and see how these ways have served you well. Then, opposite each shadow behaviour, write down what you dare not express or do up to this point in time. If you find this exercise particularly difficult and threatening, find somebody with whom you feel emotionally safe and do the exercise together. In expressing what lies hidden, start with the challenge that is least threatening and gradually work your way up to the most difficult challenge. Patience needs to accompany you on each step of your realisation of your sexual presence.

Protection	What I dare not express
'I hate my body.'	'My body is uniquely beautiful.'
'Sex is dirty.'	'Sex is wonderful.'
Ignorance	'I have a right to enjoy my body.'
'No one would find me sexually attractive.'	'I embrace fully my own sexual attractiveness.'
'My penis is not big enough.'	'Sex is about the expression of feeling, not the size of my penis.'

Rehearsal of the following affirmations may support you on your journey:

'My body is sacred.'

'Nobody looks exactly like me.'

'I embrace my unique beauty.'

'Sexual being and doing are wonderful gifts.'

'I love and care for my body.'

'Sex is great.'

'My body is wise.'

In realising our sexual presence, we honour our bodies by recognising what they are attempting to reveal to us, instead of frequently denying the knowledge that comes from a deeper and much wiser part of our being.

REALISING YOUR EMOTIONAL PRESENCE

All feelings are positive. Feelings can reach the peaks of joy and ecstasy and the depths of despair. Welfare emotions bring us into the realms of well-being, intimacy, motivation and fulfilment. Emergency feelings alert us to threats to being real. All feelings have a sacred function and deserve to be embraced and expressed.

To give and receive love is the deepest emotional need of all. Self-love is the essence of giving to and receiving from others. Knowing your worthiness to be loved by yourself and others is essential to your realising your emotional presence.

For many women, what lies hidden in terms of loving themselves is seeing themselves as worthy of receiving love. The hidden challenge for men is to see themselves as worthy of giving love. Only when you can give and receive love are you free to express fully your worthiness.

The spontaneous expression of worth, kindness, compassion,

optimism and joy are part of fully being in your emotional presence. It is vital that love and other welfare feelings are unconditionally expressed, and do not harbour conditional or manipulative agendas. In their wisdom the people at the receiving end of manipulative emotional expression will detect the covert motivation and counter the threat with a closing-down of emotional receptivity.

It is not only welfare feelings that lie hidden. Experience has led both men and women to hide certain emergency feelings as well. Women tend to mask their feelings of anger, resentment, bitterness and rage, while men tend to mask their emergency feelings of fear, anxiety, vulnerability, depression and feeling threatened. Both genders need to take on the challenge of expressing their taboo feelings if they are to feel fully alive.

The crucial issue is that your emotional expression of self does not pose a threat to either the presence of yourself or another. When you own your feelings and express them in an 'I' message, so that you show full responsibility for what you are feeling, then your emotional expression is unlikely to threaten another; if it does, then the other person is not ready to receive your openness. Examples of 'I' messages are: 'I love you'; 'You are special to me'; 'I worry when you don't call'; 'I feel fearful when you start shouting at me.'

Some affirmations that may support the expression of your emotional presence are:

'I unconditionally love myself and others.'
'All feelings are positive.'
'Listening to my internal emotional world is vital to my well-being.'
'In expressing my feelings I am being true to myself and others.'

'Emergency feelings challenge me to be true to myself.'
'Emergency feelings are my allies, alerting me to care for myself and others.'
'Feelings never lie.'

REALISING YOUR INTELLECTUAL PRESENCE

You have been given enormous intellectual capacity to comprehend and survive in the worlds in which you live. Many people are labelled 'slow' or 'weak' or 'average', but such labels reflect the vulnerability around the intellectual capacity of the labeller. You may lack competence in certain knowledge fields – and there is no one who does not – but knowledge and intelligence are not the same. Intelligence is a potential that is a given; knowledge is acquired. Because life is short we may only get to explore some knowledge areas, but what an amazing adventure that can be.

The key issue is not whether you can learn, but whether you are motivated to learn and willing to apply the required learning effort. If you have lost the drive to learn, then there are experiences in your past that have led you to hide your natural curiosity and eagerness to learn. It would help to recall these experiences, the labels that were put on you and the protective ways you developed to hide your unique intellectual potential and giftedness. What is true of your intellectual presence is the opposite of all the shadowed messages that you received from others and that you protectively applied to yourself.

Listening, reading, exploring, inventing, developing, imagining, dreaming, remembering, examining, being constructively critical, writing and composing are all ways of getting into your intellectual presence. Being determined to pursue educational courses is an additional step you could take along the road to realising your intellectual potential.

Practice of affirmations that reflect your intellectual power and unique giftedness may aid your intellectual realisation of self:

'I have been given limitless intellectual potential.'
'I have the ability to make sense and order out of the world I live in.'
'I possess a unique giftedness.'
'Nobody sees the world in exactly the same way as I do.'
'I have the ability to understand my own and others' protective and real behaviours.'
'I have all the ability to learn more and more about myself, others and the world.'
'All my thoughts have meaning.'
'Learning is an adventure.'

REALISING YOUR BEHAVIOURAL PRESENCE

Behaviour is the expression of how we intellectually perceive ourselves, others and the world — emotionally, sexually and spiritually. Generally speaking, the repertoire of knowledge and skills you presently possess are a fair representation of the expectations that the significant people in your life and the surrounding cultures have of you. The more expansive our repertoire of behaviours, the more likely it is that we were encouraged strongly to risk-take and take responsibility for our own lives, or that in our adulthood we have freed ourselves of our fears.

As adults we need no longer be dependent on others or cultures that darken our presence. In attempting to free ourselves we create a platform for developing those behaviours and skills in areas that attract and impress us. Also we need to identify those behavioural responses that we dare not show and give ourselves the permission here and now to bring those behaviours into the light of day. There is nothing we cannot do, no behaviour we cannot develop; and when you apply all your potential and giftedness you will enjoy and progress in your chosen ambitions.

Greet failure and success as stepping stones to further learning and have no desire to prove yourself to anyone or any culture. In your new-found freedom, spontaneity and adventurous spirit, support the mature progress of others and the social systems in which you participate, rather than letting them block you. You do not turn a blind eye to blows to your or others' worth, and you will assert strongly the rights of all.

You know that every behaviour you engage in has meaning and, rather than judging and condemning behaviours that darken your or others' presence, you seize the opportunity to realise what is hidden.

Some affirmations that may support you in tapping into your behavioural potential are:

'My behaviour always makes sense.'
'I possess the potential to develop the knowledge and skills to explore all aspects of the world.'
'I embrace failure and success as intrinsic to all learning.'
'I know that fear of failure and addiction to success are very serious blocks to progress.'
'I know that my behaviour is only a means of exploration and is in no way any measure of mine or others' worth.'
'I embrace the adventure of life.'
'I will keep a balance between being and doing.'

At times the most important behaviour is to do nothing. The realisation that I do not have to do anything to prove myself is powerful and creative, but it is a pursuit that most people run from. Doing and having have become the sinister enemies of maturity, being and spirituality. By freeing yourself of all the ways you have tried to gain approval, you discover your immense power.

REALISING YOUR SOCIAL PRESENCE

There are few of us whose presence has not been demeaned, lessened, marginalised, dismissed and ignored. Anonymity, social inferiority and social phobia are some of the end protectors of such darkening experiences. In the realisation of your social presence, you find your independence, your reliance on yourself, so you can fully bring your presence to all social events.

It is for you to realise that awesome and powerful presence and to stay in your presence no matter whom you are with or what social system you frequent. Silently affirm your special presence before, as you enter, during and after social situations. When anybody attempts to shadow your presence, you verbally assert your worthiness, and when this does not gain you respect, you take whatever mature action is required for you to maintain your dignity. You stay only in social situations that are worthy of your dignity. Clearly, the nature, frequency, intensity and durability of the blows to your presence will be important determinants of your decision to confront an untenable situation. What is essential is that you do not dilute your presence or dignity for the sake of acceptance from others or inclusion in an unenlightened culture.

Some affirmations that may help you to come closer to your unique social presence are:

'I am special.'
'Difference is what distinguishes me from everybody else.'
'My wish is to stay true to my own unique nature.'
'I will only accept that which is worthy of my dignity.'
'In a world of individuals it makes no sense to compare.'

REALISING YOUR CREATIVE PRESENCE

Both individuals themselves and society lose out when individuals employ their vast creativity and giftedness to guard themselves against blows to their unique presence. It is also true to say that social systems that are largely protective in nature do not benefit the individual or society at large. Sadly, that is the reality, but it is a fact which both individuals and cultures do not face. Delusion, not realism, is the bricks and mortar of the lives of most people and social systems.

You are here to live your own unique life in a way that is individual, creative and not threatening to the light of others. Individuality, difference and creativity can be a threat to people and cultures in shadow, but in realising yourself you can no longer 'hide your light under a bushel'; you serve neither yourself nor anybody else.

The fostering and support of individuality and creativity ensures personal and interpersonal maturity and societal progress.

It helps to seek support from other like-minded people when going against the tide of sameness that can seem over-whelming. Seek out people and sub-cultures that are life-giving and that celebrate individuality and creativity.

Whether or not there is support for your creative expression of self, in all dimensions of your being and doing, it is for you to take up your right to live your life as you would wish.

Affirmations may help to remind you of the uniqueness, individuality and creativity that are integral to your nature:

'I am here to live my own life.'
'Nobody experiences the world in the way that I do.'
'Resistance to conformity is going to mark my living from now on.'
'I acknowledge how creative my shadow world is but now I am going to employ my creativity to express my light.'
'My living is going to be a creative adventure.'

REALISING YOUR SPIRITUAL PRESENCE

Realising your spiritual presence is the culmination of the expression of all aspects of your real self and how powerful you are at hiding your sacred self from dark forces. When you feel your worthiness and uniqueness and see the wisdom of your body and mind, you experience the light of your being. Living in the light carries the practice of loving kindness towards yourself and others. Primarily it is through the spirit that you invest in your everyday behaviours that you realise your spiritual presence. Retreat and reflection are also essential to realising your spiritual presence. There is no suggestion here that you retreat to a monastery, but what is recommended is daily practice of quiet time to consider the activities of your day, the thoughts that occupied your mind, the feelings that touched your heart, and the dreams that entered your sleep. Keeping a daily diary of your thoughts and dreams keeps you in touch with the progress you are making in the realisation of self. Realising your spiritual presence needs time, attention, reflection, routine and commitment.

Spirituality is also about transcendence, and sometimes in the experiencing of the fullness of your light you experience an encompassing peacefulness and an interconnectedness between all things. This non-sensory experience fosters a deeper care for self, others, other species and the environment. Going to a local park, visiting a scenic area, enjoying a particular painting that inspires you, or reading spiritual teachings that uplift you, are other ways that may help you to focus on realising your spiritual presence.

Spirituality also asks the deeper questions about soul, the existence of God, immortality, the meaning of life and the nature of good and evil. Whilst some of these issues have been touched on here, others are beyond the scope of this book. However, I do believe that the realisation of self is the foundation of all spirituality.

LISTENING TO YOUR OWN INNER VOICE

The wisdom of your psyche knows your worth, sacredness and giftedness and strives at all times to communicate to you what is blocking your light and what will help you to realise yourself. Intuition is the voice of this wisdom, which was there from the beginning and precedes all learning. Intuition is a knowing that operates with data beyond sensory perception.

Intuition is revealed in the hunch about danger, the 'gut' reaction, the attraction to a certain person, work or book; it is the sense that a new idea that has never been tried before might work; it is the sudden answer to a question, the light that comes out of the darkness of confusion.

In the same way that we can learn to discipline the mind, we can learn to develop and employ intuition. One important way to encourage intuition is to get into the habit of resolving internal and external emotional conflicts by the end of each day so you do not go to bed in anger, sadness or bitterness, or weighed down by the emotional issues of others. Deep relaxation and meditative practices also help the development of intuition. You need to be willing to hear what your intuition is saying to you and act accordingly.

Intuition rests on the realisation that there is a reason for all that happens in our lives and that reason is always compassionate and good.

The guidance that humans receive through intuitive processes is as essential for their own well-being and growth as are sunshine and clean air. The answers that come through your intuition can often challenge what consciously you might prefer to do, and can be contaminated by fears. For example, parents understand intuitively that they need to hold their children's happiness at heart, but the way they interpret that need can be influenced by their insecurities. Slapping children 'for their own good' is a contaminated intuition, which on closer scrutiny reveals the need for the parents to control their children so that they will not be seen by others to be poor at parenting.

EXPLORING THE EXPANSIVENESS OF BEING YOURSELF

There is no limit to your interior world. Use any voice that helps you to touch into your amazing self — music, nature, poetry, art, scripture, meditation, stillness, movement, dance, metaphor, dreams, fantasy, thought, action, listening, athletics, relationships. The more you touch into the expansiveness of your real self, the more you will bring wisdom, love, compassion, creativity, intelligence and productivity to the cultures of which you are a member.

CONFRONTING PEOPLE WHO DARKEN YOUR PRESENCE

The road less travelled is the path back to self, the path towards realising your light and liberating your self from the shadows of fear, dependence, competitiveness, stress, delusion and depression. The road most trodden is the path away from self, that dark odyssey where you are compelled to hide your light and, in turn, block others from realising their unique selves.

Like so many other actions towards others, confronting those who cast shadows on your presence starts with confronting your own actions. Only when you are in the process of taking responsibility for your own sacred life can you confront others.

Confrontation is not about blaming others, nor is it an attempt to control or change others. On the contrary, it is about taking action for yourself in the face of behaviours from others that threaten or lessen your presence. When you embark on your journey of liberating the self, there will be many who will do all in their power to entice you back to your and their shadowed ways. Lovers, spouses, friends, parents, children, professionals, colleagues or clerics may attempt to thwart your quest. Their blocking responses reflect their shadow selves; your changing attitudes and behaviours threaten the walls of their fortresses. It is not for you to judge or counter-threaten — these reactions will only serve to escalate the situation and put you in the situation of employing shadow behaviours. The nature of your confrontation needs to be action that keeps you on your enlightened path. For example, if your partner should ridicule your efforts — meditation, personal development course, reading of books on psycho-spirituality, making decisions for yourself — your confrontation would involve continuing your enlightened behaviour and not allowing yourself to be taken off your path. It is not your partner you need to convince, but yourself. If your partner is open to reasonable and respectful discussion, then certainly respond to his or her doubts, questions and anxieties. However, be wary of taking responsibility for his or her insecurities. Listen, offer support but be clear within yourself that you are going to remain true to yourself. Should your partner's attempts to control you take on an aggressive turn — physical or verbal — you will then need to take stronger actions to maintain your freedom. This may mean breaking the silence on the aggression, seeking support from others, taking space within or outside the relationship, legal action. None of these confrontations are aimed at changing your partner's protective ways, but are strong actions towards the realisation of yourself. Paradoxically, these actions make it more likely that your partner will find some solid ground to make a step in the direction of the road less travelled.

Sometimes a group (family, work colleagues, religious community, peer group) will attempt to block your journey. Difficult decisions and action may need to be taken to ensure your progress towards realisation of self, but be assured that the only action you will truly regret is the one that brings you back into your shadowed world. I have encountered young men and women who have endured all sorts of emotional and material threats to living their own independent lives. Their parents threatened 'cutting them off from their legacy' and, even more sadly, 'stopping all contact with them unless they conformed'. Wisely the young people found support outside the family to continue their exciting personal journey. In most cases their families eventually accepted and respected their being true to themselves.

CONFRONTING CULTURES THAT DARKEN YOUR PRESENCE

When a major social system (school, workplace, community, church, country) becomes a block to your journey and threatens serious consequences should you persist in your non-conformity, then confrontation is a very difficult challenge. The threats you may be exposed to may take the form of loss of job, ostracisation, physical violence, public ridicule, dismissal of your beliefs, anonymity. Difficult decisions are required in the face of such controlling forces. Sometimes the decision to move out from a particular dark culture is what is needed. Many people have chosen to leave communities torn apart by political differences and religious bigotry and find a community that is respectful of people's differences. Similarly, individuals and families flee from countries with militaristic regimes that torture and exploit their people. Individuals choose to leave workplaces that are demeaning of workers' presence. Sometimes a delay in decision-making may be necessary until the time is right. For example, in a prosperous country, moving from a dark work-place is easier than in a country where unemployment is high.

Joining groups that oppose neglectful regimes and attempt to create more enlightened social systems is always a way forward. Also creating friendships with like-minded individuals who are also presently 'stuck' in shadowed cultures helps to maintain your sights on realising self.

STAYING SEPARATE FROM THE SHADOW BEHAVIOURS OF OTHERS

The shadow behaviour of others is about them and not about you. However, when you are in the shadow place of dependence on someone, you will interpret his or her shadow responses as being about you, and you will either conform or rebel. The more you come to a place of independence, the more you stay separate from the shadow behaviour of others. You do this by holding on to your solid sense of self and not allowing yourself to become engulfed in the shadow world of others. In this process you stay in a caring place for yourself and for the person in shadow. When you personalise another person's protective behaviours, communication breaks down immediately; you have gone into shadow and the other person stays in shadow – no progress can be made. When you stay in the light of your own presence, you understand and have compassion in a way that provides the opportunity for the other person to come into authenticity.

An example will help clarify this enlightening process. Your partner complains 'You always get your own way.' Staying separate from this shadow behaviour, you respond 'Tony, in what way do you feel I always get my own way?' Your partner responds, 'Well, we always do what you want and go where you want to go.' The temptation is to say, 'Well, you never can make up your mind and somebody has to decide.' However, that would be reacting and so you maturely answer: 'I'm sorry you feel that way and I would like to know what your preferences are.' Because you have not conformed ('Of course, you're right, I didn't see I was doing this') or rebelled ('Somebody has to make decisions around here'), you have created a degree of emotional safety for your partner to realise that he has an opportunity to own his needs. He may now reply 'I can see that I need to express my own needs more clearly'. Your response of 'I would like that' further reinforces the open communication that has emerged.

When your partner persists in his shadow response, it is crucial you continue to stay separate and assert positively: 'I am willing to listen to your needs but not take responsibility for them.'

SEEKING SUPPORT FOR YOUR JOURNEY

The journey inwards is the road to the expression of the fullness of your being and living from the inside out. Realising self means journeying against the tide of inter-personal and cultural forces that want you to remain in shadow. These forces can be overwhelming, and it is import-ant that you seek support for the journey. People in deep shadow are not supportive of those who begin to travel the road to realising self. On the contrary, subconsciously they will do all in their shadow power to block that progress, not because they want to prevent your realisation of self, but because they are dependent on you being a certain way. Most relationships — intimate, familial, friends, work, com-munity or even casual — tend to be co-dependent and any move towards maturity on the part of one of the parties threatens that co-dependent balance.

Sometimes the last place you will find support for your journey is from within your family of origin and intimate relationships. This is not surprising, as very often the sources of your shadow selves lie in your family of origin, and frequently your spouse or partner is like the parent whose own shadow world darkened your presence.

It makes a tremendous difference when support does come

from important relationships in your life. Asking for support does not mean you are looking for somebody to take over for you. What you require is the encouragement to keep to your difficult task and the understanding that this inner process is going to change how you live your life. There will be times when you will allow yourself to feel the full impact of your shadow selves, and understanding and support during those times of hurt, anger, depression, loneliness, rage and despair are essential. Sometimes you may need the support of a professional helper. It is important that such a helper can be fully present to your internal process and understands the impact that your biographical history has had on your journey to realising self. Crucially, the helper you choose needs to be one who trusts the wisdom of the shadow selves that you created to guard your sacred presence.

Seek out individuals who themselves are on the journey of self-realisation and enlightened sub-cultures – person-centred workplaces, personal and social development courses, community care groups, spiritual teachings, meditation and yoga groups. Support can also be found in reading books or listening to tapes or watching particular films or videos that inspire you. You may also find support in having a place to go to that you associate with security, safety and peace – by the sea, in a forest, in a church, on a mountain, by a lake, in a garden, in a particular room, looking at a particular view.

As you progress towards realising your self, you will find that your perspective will change on relationships, work, community, religion, education, health and well-being. You will also begin to attract different people and experiences into your life, all of which will be supportive of your own journey.

CHAPTER TEN
ENLIGHTENED CULTURES

NO PERSON IS AN ISLAND

The baby in the womb is profoundly affected by the physical, psychological and social well-being of its mother. The womb is the first culture that a human being inhabits, and this membership of cultures will continue to the time of death, and some believe, after death as well. So many of our needs are met through relationships. Children are highly dependent on their parents, and the nature of their parents' relationships to them will deeply affect how they see all aspects of themselves. Neither must the influence of relatives, neighbours, babysitters and child-minders be underestimated. Nowadays, child-minders spend more time with children than do parents, and the effects of childminders on children has yet to be documented. What is certain is that if the nature of the child-minder's relationship with children in any way darkens any aspect of their presence, then its effect will be plain to those who are ready to see. Sadly, some parents are so caught up in their careers or with each other that they miss the signs of their children exhibiting false personas in response to threats to their being real. What also requires close supervision is children's relationships to each other, and there are many children whose presence is dominated by other siblings.

By the time children arrive, their parents are involved in many relationships and are members of different social systems, and the quality of these connections will have a large influence on how each parent relates to each child. Parents' relationships with each other, family of origin, friends, neighbours, work colleagues, priests, teachers will determine many agendas of the parenting that children receive. Over-involvement or under-involvement in any of these relationships can affect children's sense of themselves. Of course, there are parents who are isolated from each other, and from all others, or who are in serious conflict, leading to a drastically unstable home environment for children. The effect of such a home culture is children having to hide their sacred selves behind virtually impenetrable battlements.

Children need parents to respond to their physical, emotional, social, sexual, intellectual, sensual, creative, recreational and spiritual needs. Later on they will reach beyond the home to teachers, relatives, peer group, neighbours, politicians, work organisations, for the further realisation of themselves. As teenagers their need to be included in their peer group is essential; later on the need for a same-sex bosom pal emerges, and further down the line, the need for intimacy with another young adult healthily evolves. However, what is now well known is that how and whether or not children exhibit these developments will be strongly determined by what they witnessed in their earlier relationships. For example, a family that sticks together and allows no connections with outsiders will result in children not going through the developmental stages of creating relationships outside the home.

As young adults, the challenges of ongoing education, career development, adult-adult relationships will arise, whether or not they are ready to take on such responsibilities. And the sad fact is that many young people, because of the limitations of past and present relationships and cultures, are often not ready for adult responsibilities. However, this does not stop them from getting into serious relationships, marriage or parenthood. This lack of readiness and premature adoption of major adult roles frequently means that the cycle of neglectful relationships begins all over again. Only when a member of the present generation reflects on and resolves a diminished view of self and others will the buck stop.

The foregoing shows that the key to creating enlightened cultures is establishing stable and unconditional relationships from the very start of a child's life. Intimacy is the *sine qua non* for an effective and caring culture.

THE ESSENCE OF ENLIGHTENED CULTURES

It may be simple to say that the essence of enlightenment is unconditional love, but saying and doing are two entirely different things. There is no doubt that the cause of all human problems can be traced to a lack of loving, but such neglect can be perpetrated in unlimited ways. Knowing what leads to individuals hiding their real presence is as important as seeing what are the factors that lead to people holding onto their unique selves. Certainly, the absence of behaviours that lessen people's sense of self and the presence of unconditional love lie at the heart of enlightened cultures. It is through the relationship within each individual and between individuals that unconditional intimacy is shown.

A person does not have to be loved by another in order to know what love is, but I believe that the experience of receiving and giving love is a necessary prerequisite to loving self. In the darkened era of dominant religious cultures, the best kept secret was that one should love oneself. Indeed, any such self-adoration would have been horribly punished and the person branded as 'selfish', 'sinful', 'bad', 'evil', 'vain' and 'narcissistic'. There was cleverness in that darkened culture, as the Church subconsciously knew that the love of self leads to power beyond measure. It was not the Church's aim to inspire their congregation with a celebration of their sacredness, but to control with threats of judgment, domination and hell-fire. Even today the effects of such violations of the human spirit can be heard in the shadow responses to the challenge to embrace self: 'How do I love myself?'; 'I don't understand what you mean to have a relationship with myself'; 'Isn't that so selfish?' Ironically, selfishness arises from people not loving themselves and their attempt to fill their inner void either by 'I am nothing, so please let me live my life for you', or 'I am nothing, so please live your life for me'. Such enmeshed and co-dependent relationships are still too common.

There are many individuals who for protective reasons have gone off the path to the realisation of self and have found substitute ways of filling the inner void of distance from their real selves. A substitute can be any substance or action — alcohol, food, work, relationships, success, gambling, sickness, religion, drugs, sports.

It is important that each culture concretises what intimacy means for its members. The leaders of all cultures have a duty to determine the needs of its members and to set up structures and resources that ensure appropriate responses to declared needs. Whether resources are limited or unlimited, transparency is needed so that fair allocation to all members is visible. Leaders have an even greater responsibility to examine their own inner culture, since the main source of enlightened leadership is personal authenticity. There are too many instances of neglect, not only in the political history, but in the violations suffered by individuals in family, school, church, work cultures and welfare institutions. Leaders who possess a darkened sense of self only cast shadows on those for whom they have responsibility. It is for this reason that leaders (for example, parents, teachers, politicians, child-minders, sports trainers, managers, entrepreneurs, medical doctors, nurses, medical consultants, clinical psychologists, counsellors, social workers) require preparation for their significant roles in society. Regrettably, most leaders do not receive such training. The training would need to involve not only an explanation of the inner world of self but also an exploration of how the person and rights and needs of others are viewed.

There is the assumption that a person who has an enlightened view of self will automatically be concerned about the welfare of others. This is a psychological fallacy, because the social, educational, intellectual, spiritual, career, physical and political development of individuals and groups are far too complex and require an in-depth knowledge of social and political systems. There is a corresponding fallacy, known as the sociological fallacy, which assumes that the presence of sound social and political structures ensures personal fulfilment. An effective culture and leader knows too well the need for direct attention to both the interior and exterior worlds of each individual.

ENLIGHTENED CULTURES

An enlightened culture is one that is intimate without being invasive, caring without being crippling of an individual's autonomy, involved without being over-involved, and responsible to the inevitable economic, social, religious, educational, scientific, technological and work changes that occur. Whereas each culture has a particular role to play, all cultures should keep in mind that human beings do not present themselves in neat packages to fit into the pigeon-holes of a culture, and that a holistic eye must oversee the workings of particular cultures. Professional specialisation has resulted in the human person being broken down into distinct parts, so that those practitioners who stick rigidly to a tunnel vision of human behaviour very often do not know what their left hand is doing. For example, work cultures tend to see workers as resources (hence 'human resources management') and miss the fact that workers do not leave their individual, familial, social, religious and cultural needs or baggage outside the workplace door. Work organisations that lose sight of the total person pile up untold problems for themselves and for their employees. Similarly, the school that believes education is only about the development of cognitive and work skills is neglectful of students' and staff's physical, emotional, social, sexual and spiritual growth.

THE ENLIGHTENED FAMILY CULTURE

The foundation for the enlightened family is the parent's own possession of self and independence of others. Independence does not mean a lack of recognition of the interconnectedness that exists between individuals and social systems. What it does mean is that informed decisions will be made on the rightness of the beliefs, assumptions, traditions and values of the culture(s) of which one is a member. Conformity to the norms and values of a culture does not evolve from a serious analysis of its functioning. Each member (and especially leaders) of a culture needs to listen to his or her inner voice and test whether or not the handed-down beliefs and practices match intuition; if not, difficult decisions may need to be made.

A parent has a duty to love self and others, and from that solid base to identify and respond to the drive in each child to realise their enormous potential and giftedness. Individuality is the cornerstone of the mature family, and the parents who have real-ised this in themselves are in a powerful position to foster a similar emergence in their children. However, parents also need to recognise that children will need to adapt to the various cultures they will encounter and that preparation and education for entry to these social systems will be required. The most effective way to prepare children for the world beyond home is the modelling by parents of the beliefs and actions needed to adjust to and thrive in these systems. Parents would do well to acquaint children with the dark side of these cultures and provide them with the independence, discriminatory power and assertiveness to resist aspects of cultures that can threaten the realisation of self.

Within the home, the enlightened family system is seen as the place that provides for the holistic development of each member, and no one member is more important than another. For too long fathers were given too central a place in the family, even though it was mothers who carried at least 90 per cent of the parenting role. Many women have a tendency to postpone their own development for the sake of their children. However, this is not good practice. Male children too often develop a sense of importance beyond that of female children, arising from the family that revolves around the father, and there is also the situation where female children repeat the pattern of their mothers by putting all else before self.

There are serious issues confronting the nature of family in contemporary society. Lone parenting, single-parenting arising from separation or divorce, same-sex two parent-families, joint-parenting families (parents separated), second-marriage families with children from the first marriage as well as newly born children to the newly married couple. The rise of fatherless families is a worrying trend. Some women might claim that women always did the parenting anyway, so what is new? *Touché*! But research shows that there is nothing to compare to the stable two-parent family. This makes sense, as parenting is a difficult profession and the sharing of it between two responsible adults must add to its effectiveness. The trend towards fatherless families needs to be seriously addressed by governments, social agencies and churches. Men need to be supported and encouraged to take on an equal share of the parenting of their children. Furthermore, the polarisation of males and females is not beneficial to anyone's progress; neither within men nor women is the polarisation of masculinity and femininity desirable. Both men and women have a duty to come into the fullness of their unique presence and this means the embracing of both aspects of self — feminine and masculine. It has been unfortunate that masculinity has become associated with men and femininity with women. For women and men to come fully into their own interiority and to be effective leaders of the family, both must embrace the full expansiveness of human characteristics. For a man to develop his feminine side does not mean losing any aspect of his maleness. Similarly, for a woman to explore her masculine side does not in any way take from her femaleness. The fully rounded person and mature parent possesses both sets of characteristics.

MASCULINE CHARACTERISTICS	FEMININE CHARACTERISTICS
▢ ambition	▢ compassion
▢ assertiveness	▢ emotional expression
▢ determination	▢ emotional receptivity
▢ drive	▢ intuition
▢ initiative	▢ kindness
▢ logic	▢ listening
▢ order	▢ nurturance
▢ physical strength	▢ sensitivity
▢ power	▢ tenderness
▢ self-control	▢ understanding

An intimate family culture makes a definite distinction between person and behaviour. The parent-architects know that their own and their children's sacred selves are always unconditional and worthy of unconditional love, that no behaviour either adds or detracts from their person. This is a difficult pill for many parents to swallow, because their own experience in their family culture and other cultures was that their behaviour was a measure of their worth. However, such conditionality breeds insecurity and holds back the realisation of self. Each individual desires to be loved for self, and on this issue there is no such thing as benign neglect. Behaviour is a person's way of exploring interior and exterior worlds, but must never become a yardstick of a person's worth. Ironically, parents will be far more effective in helping children to take on responsible behaviours when there is no confusion between person and behaviour. The security of knowing that you are loved for yourself provides the solid ground from which nobody can demean, exile or exclude you, and the adventure and challenge of learning poses no threat and can be embraced fully. Infants have a wonderful natural curiosity and eagerness to learn; this is frequently extinguished or reduced by parents living their lives through their children's achievements and 'good' behaviours, or by the harsh punishment and withdrawal of love when children do not conform to parental expectations. People are not their behaviour and this vital issue is central to the well-being of the family.

Parenting is a profession that goes beyond the essential task of unconditionally loving children. It also entails helping children to explore their inner and outer worlds and to learn to live peacefully with themselves and with others. This complex brief means that parents need to understand the nature of their own and their children's physical, sexual, emotional, social, intellectual, educational, behavioural, occupational, recreational and spiritual development. The sad fact is that few parents are prepared for the enormous responsibility of parenting and it is a gross neglect of society not to have training structures in place for aspiring parents. Real progress will happen when parenting is seen as the core profession in society. There is no suggestion that parenting training courses will solve all of society's problems, but they will certainly considerably reduce them. Effective parenting courses will need to focus not only on the child's develop-ment but also on resolving the emotional baggage that parents bring to their role as family architects. Much of this baggage is subconscious, and it is incumbent on others who witness children being neglected by parents who are in a shadowed place, to assert the need for those parents to seek the help they most obviously require. This is not an easy task, and indeed, can be a dangerous responsibility to take on. The principle is to find a means of confrontation that is non-threatening to your own and to the children's welfare.

The rising tide of marital breakdown does not mean that

family breakdown has to follow. However, when the couple in conflict do not resolve their differences amicably and fairly, then children suffer. Each parent needs to hold onto the fact that an untenable marital relationship need not jeopardise their parenting and family responsibilities. Again, these are difficult issues to handle maturely and parents in the sad situation of marriage failure need all the help they can get. The deeper reason why a marriage or long-term relationship ends in conflict needs to be sought by each partner so that the pattern of neglect, disappointment and hurt is not repeated. Whether an individual is in a single or lone or shared parenting role, the living peacefully with self is the basis of effective parenting. In other words, all parenting starts with self.

CHARACTERISTICS OF AN ENLIGHTENED FAMILY

- ☐ Unconditional love
- ☐ Parent at peace with self
- ☐ Couple harmony
- ☐ Non-possessive warmth and affection
- ☐ Non-judgmental attitude
- ☐ Separation of person and behaviour
- ☐ Demonstration of a love of others and of life
- ☐ Regular affirmation of the uniqueness, individuality, worth, lovability and capability of each family member
- ☐ Sensitivity to and encouragement of each family member's special interests, hobbies and ways of doing things
- ☐ Acceptance of each other
- ☐ Respect and value for each other
- ☐ Acknowledgment of strengths and vulnerabilities
- ☐ An interest in each other's lives

- Active listening
- Encouragement and praise of behavioural efforts
- Positive firmness with regard to being responsible, and positive correction when not responsible
- Family relationships neither threatened nor broken because of shadow responses
- Genuineness and realness in interactions with one another
- Fostering of independence
- Nurturing of creativity
- Fostering of a love of learning and challenge
- Mistakes and failures seen as opportunities for learning

ENLIGHTENED SCHOOL CULTURES

Every school comprises the individual presence of each person as well as the collective presence of all the members of the school. One of the major difficulties with a school culture is that each classroom can also be a culture unto itself and not reflect the pattern of the wider school culture. In a situation where the school culture lessens the presence of its members, sometimes an individual teacher's classroom can be an oasis in the desert of an uncaring school culture. However, where the opposite occurs, confusion and frustration can reign and students, in particular, can become distressed because of the lack of consistency in caring, respect and definite fair boundaries.

Other teachers can also become resentful at the uncooperative and deleterious influence of those teachers who prove resistant to any demands for cooperative behaviour. The architect of a school culture is the school principal, and his or her leadership style is a significant determinant of the quality of a school culture. To date, strong measures have not tended to be employed to bring about harmony in the school culture, but this is neglectful, not only of those members in distress, but also of the principals, teachers and students who are the source of the distress. Both principals and teachers have a major responsibility to ensure that their interactions with each other and with students are of a nature that honours the presence of each member of the school culture. Below is a self-observation checklist of behaviours that are the hallmarks of professional effectiveness: it can be used to determine present strengths and challenges. Any shortcomings provide the opportunities for further professional and personal development. It is crucial that the school culture looks on shortcomings in a positive way, rather than making it threatening for a principal or a teacher to identify and seek help and support on a particular professional incompetence. There are many teachers who live in fear of judgment and condemnation and are thereby forced to cover up areas of teaching where they are less than competent.

A self-monitoring checklist can include the following:

- ☐ Do I like students?
- ☐ Do I respect students?
- ☐ Do I address students by their first names?
- ☐ Am I challenged by teaching?
- ☐ Do I respond to failure and success as equal and integral parts of learning?
- ☐ Do I put emphasis on learning as an adventure and not as a pressure to perform?
- ☐ Do I correct positively students' schoolwork and homework?
- ☐ Do I arrive on time for class?
- ☐ Do I have definite boundaries around respect for self and others?

- ☐ Do I communicate directly and clearly what is required of students in and out of classrooms?
- ☐ Do I listen to students?
- ☐ Am I firm and do I take definitive action when violations of the rights of teachers and students occur?
- ☐ Do I maintain understanding for the student who presents classroom difficulties whilst being clear that his or her problem behaviours cannot be allowed to be sources of violations of other people's rights?
- ☐ Do I seek back-up support when needed?
- ☐ Do I liaise with parents at the early signs of difficulties?
- ☐ Is my sense of self separate from what I do?
- ☐ Does my teaching approach inspire or threaten students?
- ☐ Do I accept and celebrate the uniqueness and individuality of each student?
- ☐ When under stress do I seek solutions?

The above list is by no means exhaustive and it is advisable that each school devise its own checklist to reflect the responsibilities that are peculiar to the school setting. Nevertheless, there are common issues that individual teachers need to address in evaluating their teaching style; these revolve around their own sense of self, their attitude to education and to failure and success, their cooperation with management and fellow members of staff, their relationship with students and parents, and their response to students' learning efforts and difficulties.

It benefits teachers when students and parents are aware of the above list of responsibilities so that parents, in particular, can support teachers to meet their obligations. When parents (and students) witness a falling short of what is desirable, it is incumbent on them to confront the teacher and request that the teacher take on the challenges to improving competency. In the same way that a student's emotional and behavioural difficulties cannot be allowed to block or violate the rights of other students and teachers, so too the shadow behaviours of teachers cannot become a block to students' learning and emotional and social development.

A means of evaluating the culture of the school complements the individual teacher's self-assessment. The school has a duty to ensure that its members are cherished, challenged and fairly treated. Whilst acknowledging that each school culture is a unique phenomenon, there are certain fundamental aspects to all caring school cultures.

CHARACTERISTICS OF AN ENLIGHTENED SCHOOL CULTURE

- Person-centred (rather than programme-centred)
- Relationships given priority
- Learning and teaching known to be directly related to how student and teacher feel about themselves
- Presence and absence of each school member matters
- Discipline system for all (not just students)
- Group decision-making
- Emphasis on educational effort rather than academic performance
- Mistakes and failures seen as opportunities for learning
- Success and failure viewed as relative terms
- Intelligence and knowledge seen as separate issues
- Learning has only positive associations
- Listening to the needs of all members
- Back-up support system to deal with neglect of any member
- Openness to change
- Freedom to be different
- Management style that is transformational in nature

Implementation of the above recommendations goes a long way to creating a school culture that reaches out with heart and mind to all its members.

ENLIGHTENED RELIGIOUS CULTURES

An enlightened religious culture knows and affirms the sacredness of every human being, whether or not he or she is a member of its flock. Spirituality takes expression in the unconditional loving of each and every human being and in compassion for those who are protectively out of touch with their worth and value. In the enlightened religious culture, places of worship are havens for troubled souls, where they are embraced without judgment and with non-possessive warmth, understanding and empathy.

In a positive religious culture the emphasis is on love, not law, and the efforts of pastors are directed towards helping individuals to realise their sacredness and see the worthiness of others. These pastors lead by example, not by inducing fear.

In terms of status and religious profession both men and women are deemed worthy of aspiration to these roles. The God of an enlightened religious culture does not see women or children as less than men — surely a human, but not a divine characteristic!

Pastors in the enlightened religion are champions of the poor in spirit as well as in wealth, of the oppressed, the marginalised, the sick, the dying and those in despair. This church is the lighthouse whose beacon provides the safe way for those in a dark, troubled and treacherous sea.

CHARACTERISTICS OF AN ENLIGHTENED RELIGIOUS CULTURE

- See each human being as sacred
- Unconditional love
- Foster individuality
- Tolerance of difference
- Acceptance and respect for all men, women and children
- Male and female pastors
- Compassion
- Non-judgmental
- Supportive
- Emphasis on love, not law
- Spiritual
- Reflective
- Champions of the disadvantaged

ENLIGHTENED WORK CULTURES

Workplaces do not have a history of being enlightened places. The enlightened work organisation has the philosophy that all its members are unique individuals with physical, sexual, emotional, intellectual, social, occupational, creative and spiritual rights and needs, and it does all in its power to listen and to respond to these needs.

It ensures that responsibility for meeting these needs is a two-way street and is firm with the employee who abrogates responsibility.

The enlightened work culture knows that its person-centred approach creates an ethos of valuing security, safety, challenge and excitement for all workers to take on the work goals of the organisation. It knows that valuing and affirming individuals takes precedence over productivity and profit. It is aware of the profound influence that the shadow selves of workers have on creativity, productivity and leadership. For that reason it attempts to foster relationships that enhance employees' and employers' sense of themselves. It provides special attention to those who feel bad about themselves and lack self-confidence. It also encourages these workers to seek the support and help required to realise their worth and potential.

The caring work organisation recognises the uniqueness, worth and limitless potential of each worker and attempts to communicate that image to them. It affirms workers' vast intellectual potential and does not confuse knowledge and skills with intellectual capacity. It embraces failure and success as equal stepping-stones in the wonderful process of work and, especially, praises work efforts and love of work. It knows too well the pitfalls in emphasising work perform-ance, deadlines and comparisons and competition with other companies.

The enlightened workplace places particular emphasis on respectful relationships between all members of staff and is swift to sanction disrespect among employees or between managers/supervisors and workers. It particularly seeks to make management enhancing of employees' welfare. For this reason the work organisation seeks always to be more powerful than its managers. It is its responsibility not only to be the watchguard of managers' functioning but also to select leaders who have at heart and head the welfare of themselves, the workers and the organisation. It knows too that managers require considerable support to carry out their difficult role, and it visibly backs the positive policies and actions of managers. The organisation knows that effective leadership goes beyond work knowledge and expertise to knowing how to relate to, motivate and understand workers and how to gain loyalty and commitment from them. For managers to create such contact, they require the solid ground of a strong sense of self, separateness from others' opinions of them and a balanced approach to work. The enlightened organisation is only too aware of the need for careful selection of managers.

The positive workplace recognises that its most valuable asset is its staff and it seeks to ensure that their work does not jeopardise their dignity and sense of worth and value.

CHARACTERISTICS OF AN ENLIGHTENED WORK CULTURE

- ☐ The provision of physical, sexual, intellectual, social, creative and spiritual safety for workers
- ☐ Recognition of the rights of workers
- ☐ Respect for each individual worker
- ☐ Back-up system to deal with neglect
- ☐ Transformational management style
- ☐ Person-centred ethos
- ☐ A clear vision of how the organisation wants the workplace to be
- ☐ Clear communication of the organisation's vision to workers
- ☐ Persistence, consistency and focus, particularly when workers show a lack of responsibility
- ☐ Empowerment of employees to work towards their individual and collective goals; the emphasis is on self-responsibility, questioning and altering limiting beliefs and the development of a sense of spiritual self
- ☐ Belief in workers' potential and provision of the right circumstances for them to apply their giftedness
- ☐ An accountability system for all members of the organisation

- Positive identification of and learning from mistakes and problems
- Direct, clear and bi-directional communication system between workers and managers/employers
- Family- and couple-friendly
- Promotion of balanced lifestyle
- Care for and opportunities for progress for those who manifest vulnerability
- Positive role in the community
- Good working conditions
- Visible appreciation of workers' efforts
- A fair wage

CHAPTER ELEVEN
LIVING YOUR OWN LIFE

Self-work lies at the heart of individual and cultural maturity; indeed, it is the essence of a healthy society. From what you have read in the foregoing pages it is clear that the resources, support and encouragement for such crucial work is still weak, and the very absence of such a positive climate can make it very frightening for an individual to risk living his or her own life. Of course, equally the presence of active threats to being real is also a major deterrent to self-work. Clearly too, the dangers to being real and authentic are on a continuum from low to extreme, and there are some social systems where it is highly dangerous to be real in an unreal world of domination, threat, violence and ostracisation for those who 'buck the system'. Fear or terror of living your own life can exist in all social systems (family, school, community, workplace, church, sports club) and in sub-cultures (ethnic groups) and in the wider culture of the country as a whole. The self knows the perils and will wisely begin to tread the path to liberation from fears only when safety abounds. It is true to say that authentic self-expression can occur between two or more individuals, but still remain hidden in group situations that are threatening to self-realisation.

Apart from the benefits to the individual who takes the road less travelled, the realisation of self has potential benefits for all individuals, social systems and cultures. The more expansively an individual lives out his or her own sacred life, the greater the potential benefits to others. Indeed, no matter how small the world you live in, when you express fully your unique presence in your daily comings and goings, you will positively affect your immediate world and may even begin to affect the world at large.

It is both an individual and collective responsibility to create the appropriate emotional, physical, sexual, intellectual, social, creative, occupational and spiritual safeties for the true self of each person to emerge. This is not an issue we can choose to treat lightly, as its neglect causes considerable pain and loss to individuals and great loss of harmony, maturity, creativity and productivity to the collective of individuals. Furthermore, self-realisation is a life-time challenge, and responsibility and opportunities to explore self and one's vast potential and giftedness need to be available at all stages of a person's life span.

Parents and teachers, in particular, need to take seriously the responsibility of self-work and to model for children living their own unique lives so that imitation of that process by their children will ensure the continuance of that inner journey. All leaders of communities, churches, industry and of countries have an increased duty to realise self, and voters need to use the ballot box to elect mature leaders.

The realisation, too, that it is not the behaviours you show that need to be changed but those you dare not show is crucial to liberate yourself from your fears. It is for you yourself to reflect deeply on your remote and immediate life circumstances and to detect what aspects of self-expression explored in this book you dare not show. Furthermore, your reflection needs to also determine the individuals, relationships, places (home, school, church, community, hospitals, medical, social and psychological agencies, government agencies) that were or are threatening to self-expression.

A complementary exercise is to determine those people and places where it is safe to be real because these can be your sources of support for further self-realisation.

Your self is precious, unique, intuitive, vastly intelligent, gifted, worthy, lovable, expansive and spiritual, and it is both your right and your responsibility to live your life from the inside out. Support for this journey can come in many forms – a book, a tape, a partner, a workplace, a teacher, a course, a friend, a group. It helps enormously when you seek out relationships, work and workplaces that are worthy of your dignity. A further aid to the recovery of self is the difficult decision to take action with regard to persons or social systems that in any way darken, demean or lessen your presence. The realisation of self is a long, exciting and sometimes painful journey, but there is no greater pain than for the self to remain hidden and not to be found. Patience is essential and there is a need for acceptance that progress is not a continuous process but one where you take steps forward and backwards along the way to realising self. Seek the support you need to begin the journey and step by step reveal your power beyond measure.